MELANIE KLEIN

MODERN MASTERS

EDITED BY frank kermode

melanie klein

hanna segal

THE VIKING PRESS | NEW YORK

To Daniel and Julia

Copyright © Hanna Segal, 1979
All rights reserved
First published in 1980 by The Viking Press
625 Madison Avenue, New York, N.Y. 10022

LIBRARY OF CONGRESS CATALOGING IN PUBLICATION DATA
Segal, Hanna.
  Melanie Klein.
  (Modern masters)
  Bibliography: p.
  Includes index.
  1. Klein, Melanie.   2. Psychoanalysts—Austria—
Biography.   3. Psychoanalysis.   4. Child analysis.
RC339.52.K43S43   150.19'5'0924 [B]   80–14056
ISBN 0–670–46474–0

Printed in the United States of America
Set in Primer

ACKNOWLEDGMENTS

Much of this book was written while I held the Sigmund Freud Memorial Visiting Professorship at University College London, and I should like to express my gratitude to the board of management for inviting me to occupy the Chair and providing me with the opportunities for work of my own that it gave.

My husband, Paul Segal; Miss Betty Joseph; Mrs. Edna O'Shaughnessy; and Professor Richard Wollheim all read the manuscript, and I am grateful to them for their most helpful criticisms and suggestions. I also wish to thank Miss Katherine Backhouse for her most valuable secretarial and editorial work and Miss Paula Kendall for helping out whenever necessary.

The Hogarth Press and the International Psycho-Analytical Library have given me permission to quote from the *Standard Edition* of Freud's works, from *Developments in Psycho-Analysis,* and from *The Writings of Melanie Klein,* for which I wish to thank them. Thanks are also due to W. W. Norton and Company, holders of the American copyright for "Civilization, and Its Discontents," for permission to quote from that work.

CONTENTS

MELANIE KLEIN

Introduction

●

1

Melanie Klein was a pupil and a follower of Freud. Through her work, at first mainly with children, she extended the area of knowledge and understanding opened up by Freud and she came to some new formulations which in certain ways developed Freud's ideas, and in others differed from his. I cannot present her work without reviewing, if only in a bare outline, some of the psychoanalytical ideas on which she based it.

By 1919, when she started her work, psychoanalytical theory had undergone a considerable evolution and Freud's theory of the psychic development was in some respects complete. There were, however, two new major theoretical formu-

The following abbreviations are used in the footnotes: *SE: The Standard Edition of the Complete Psychological Works of Sigmund Freud; Writings: The Writings of Melanie Klein; Int. J. Psycho-Anal.: International Journal of Psycho-Analysis.*

lations to come. The 1920s was one of the turning points in psychoanalytical theory. In 1920, in "Beyond the Pleasure Principle,"[1] Freud formulated his theory of the duality of the life and death instincts, and in 1923, in "The Ego and the Id,"[2] he worked out fully the structural theory of the mind in terms of the id, the ego, and the superego. Those developments led also to a change in his views on the nature of psychic conflict, anxiety, and guilt. Melanie Klein who, in her work with children, became convinced of the importance of innate aggression, was the only major follower of Freud to adopt fully his theory of the death instinct and to work out its clinical implications. She also developed further the structural theory throwing new light on the origin, composition, and functioning of the superego. Her approach to anxiety and guilt is more in keeping with Freud's later formulations than with his earlier ones.

One could say that psychoanalysis starts with Freud's discovery in his work with hysterical patients that symptoms have meaning. This led to the discovery of unconscious processes, of repression and symbolism. These discoveries are inseparable from one another. In a barest outline one could summarize Freud's view as follows: the painful or forbidden memory, impulse or phantasy is not allowed into consciousness; it is repressed, but remains dynamic in the person's unconscious and strives for expression; it finds symbolical expression in the symptom; the symptom is a compromise between the repressed ideas and feelings and the repressing forces. Freud was soon led to see that intrapsychic conflicts and compromise solutions lie not only in the domain of pathology. He discovered that dreams, a universal human phenomenon, have a structure similar to that of neurotic

[1] *SE* XVIII, pp. 7–64.
[2] *SE* XIX, pp. 12–66.

symptoms, and that repression and compromise solutions are part of human nature and development. Starting with a simple application of hypnosis, he gradually developed the psychoanalytic technique of free association and interpretation, which allowed him to study repressed thoughts and feelings, the reasons for their repression, and the various mental mechanisms for dealing with them. He found that the material repressed is predominantly of a sexual nature. (In contrast to popular misconception, he never contended that it was exclusively so.) This repressed sexuality is different from what is considered normal (that is, genital and heterosexual). It is bisexual, and of a markedly perverse polymorphous kind, including sadomasochistic, oral, anal, urethral, voyeuristic, exhibitionistic impulses corresponding to what, in adult sexual activity, would be perversions. This is so even in people who, in their conscious lives, are sexually normal. Freud came to the conclusion that there is not one simple sexual instinct, but that sexuality is a compound of component instincts deriving from various areas of the body and having various aims. In normal adult sexuality, the genital instinct and aim predominate. These polymorphous component instincts originate in infancy and childhood. The discovery of infantile sexuality was revolutionary. It is infantile sexuality that gives rise to conflicts and leads to repression and to the other defenses which he and his followers discovered later. The symptoms of the neurotic or the symbolism in dreams do not arise simply out of the repression of a contemporary adult conflict. It is the elements of the unconscious infantile sexuality expressed in the current problem which mobilize the infantile conflicts and bring about repression.

In the relatively short period of time between Freud's discoveries about the nature of hysteria and the radical departures of the early 1920s, Freud, Ferenczi, Abraham, Jones, and others made tremendous advances in mapping out the psychosexual development of the child and tracing its effects on adult personality. Although it is, of course, impossible in a short introduction to give full weight to the mass of psychoanalytical work and ideas on which Melanie Klein based her work, I shall try to indicate the context in which it evolved and shall return to some of the points already mentioned when examining in greater detail the use she made of those ideas, and particularly the ways in which she developed them or departed from them.

In sorting out the history of the component instincts, Freud established that they originate at different periods of the child's life. He called the total sexual energy libido, and he described the successive stages of libidinal development. Any instinct, according to him, has a source, an aim, and an object. The source is always a part of the body, the erotogenic zone. The aim is the discharge of a sexual tension. The object is an object appropriate for providing this satisfaction. The erotogenic zones are connected with vital functions. Thus, the oral component instinct derives from the vital function of eating, the anal and urethral from defecating and urinating, and the genital from the reproductive function. The satisfaction of the vital need gives rise to erotic arousal and pleasure, which is then sought for its own sake. The infant's first instinctual vital need is feeding, and thus the oral component instinct is the first to be aroused and the mouth is the first erotogenic zone. Sucking at the mother's breast is the starting point of the whole sexual life—"the unmatched prototype of every later sexual satisfaction, to which phantasy often enough recurs in times of need."[3] The primacy of the oral gives way to that

3 "Introductory Lectures on Psycho-Analysis," *SE* XVI, p. 314.

of the anal when the child begins to develop sphincter control. Expelling the stool, retaining it, wishing to be anally penetrated, becomes the center of the infantile sexual experience. Freud originally considered that the genital stage succeeded directly the anal, but he later added, between the anal and the genital, the phallic stage, occurring between the ages of three and six. At that stage the male child discovers his penis as the seat of tension and pleasure. He sees the phallus as the only sexual organ there is, and having no awareness of the female genital he phantasies his mother as having a penis like himself and his father—as the "phallic woman." Thus in Freud's description the development of the libido in the child has three phases: the oral, the anal, and the phallic. The genital phase, in which the sexes are properly differentiated, does not come into full force until puberty. When Freud speaks of the organization of the libido in these phases, he has in mind not only that a particular component instinct predominates in any given phase, but also that this instinct is associated with appropriate aims and objects. Thus, the aim of the oral instinct is sucking or devouring, the appropriate object being the breast. The anal component instinct aims at expelling or retaining, its appropriate object being the stool. The phallic instinct is to penetrate—the account of the phallic object is more complicated as, according to Freud, there is a long evolution of the object relationship before the appropriate object (the vagina) is discovered. The frustration of these drives gives rise to aggression, which seeks expression in similarly phase-appropriate ways. Thus, oral aggression takes the form of wishing to bite or to devour cannibalistically, anal aggression that of desiring to expel, burn, or poison with feces, phallic aggression that of a desire to cut, penetrate, and tear.

It is characteristic of the libido that it is very plastic

and can move from aim to aim and from object to object. One organ may be substituted for another and take over its functions. In phantasy, the anus can take the place of the mouth, the penis can replace the breast as an object of oral desires, the stool may substitute for a penis or for a baby, the baby can represent the penis, and so on.

Normally the libido progresses from the oral to the anal to the phallic and finally to the genital phase. But unsatisfactory experience may lead to a phenomenon called by Freud "fixation." A part of the libido gets fixated at a pre-genital stage and attached to the aims and objects of that phase. When this happens the organization at the genital stage is weak and insecure, and regression to the earlier phase—the point of fixation—easily occurs. This return to an organization belonging to a pre-genital stage is, in Freud's view, the determining factor of adult neurosis.

Sexual instincts undergo development: gradually the pre-genital instincts are repressed as genitality becomes dominant, but they never quite lose their power. Continuing in the unconscious, they undergo various vicissitudes and give rise to symptoms, sublimation, or character traits—orality may express itself in greed or, for instance, in appetite for knowledge. Anality can result in obsessional character traits or, as positive achievements, orderliness and cleanliness. Freud described the oral and anal character and Abraham and Jones added a great deal to his description. When the sexual aim of an instinct is inhibited so that it loses its sexual character, it may give rise to sublimation, a displacement from a sexual to a nonsexual aim. Thus, Freud describes a complex evolution of the sexual instincts preceding the final genital organization.

The object of the sexual desires also undergoes an evolution. In Freud's view, a proper sexual object does not begin to appear in psychic life until the late anal and phallic phase. The oral instinct first has as its object the breast, but then the breast is abandoned as a sexual object, possibly because it is not uninterruptedly available, and the infant becomes auto-erotic. It seeks satisfaction in its own body, in such activities as sucking its fingers or its lips. The instinct finds its satisfaction but appears to have no object. Auto-erotism gradually progresses to narcissism. Although the infant's or the child's own body is still the source of satisfaction, in narcissism (as distinct from auto-erotism) its own body is experienced as an object. This may seem to be a distinction without a difference, but psychologically it is not so. Narcissism is a transition between auto-erotism and the relationship with an external object. In phantasy the child can project his own body on to his object, and in that way the object becomes an object of desire—it is *cathected*. A fixation to narcissism can give rise later in life to a narcissistic object choice. The narcissistic person seeks in his partner a representation of himself and loves himself in his partner.

It is only in the phallic stage that the parents become objects of sexual desire, and this ushers in the Oedipus complex which is, as is well known, a central part of the psychoanalytical theory. The boy begins to desire as a sexual object his mother, the person who has always been the source of his comforts, pleasures, and satisfactions. He becomes aware of the sexual relation between his parents, and his desire for his mother leads to violent jealousy of his father which makes him hate him and wish him dead—like Oedipus, he wishes to kill his father in order to possess his mother. These desires conflict with both the fear and the love he has for his father, the predominant fear being that father will castrate him as a punishment for his sexual wishes. Fear of castration, above all, forces the boy to repress his sexuality toward mother and his aggression toward father.

His love for his father in that phase has also a strong sexual component. One of Freud's discoveries was that of bisexuality, the fact that all human beings have masculine and feminine sexual strivings. So in addition to the positive Oedipus complex, the boy also has a negative Oedipus complex: he desires sexually his father and his mother is his rival. He wants to be penetrated and possessed by his father, but since the fulfillment of those desires would lead to emasculation, his homosexual wishes have to be repressed as well. In normal development the repression of homosexual wishes is more complete and permanent than that of heterosexual ones.

The girl also goes through a phallic phase. According to Freud, she has no awareness of the vagina, and her clitoris is the leading erotogenic zone, similar to the penis. The little girl's Oedipus complex, in his account, diverges in many particulars from that of the boy, and I shall discuss this in more detail when I consider the difference between his views and those of Melanie Klein.

The Oedipus complex is a turning point in the individual's development. It is in relation to the Oedipus complex that repression sets in, and that, as a defense against Oedipal anxieties, regression occurs to pre-genital phases. All children at this moment go through a transient neurosis—the infantile neurosis—developing, in response to the Oedipal situation, defenses which lead to the formation of phobias, obsessions, and other symptoms. Adult neurosis is a regression to this infantile neurosis.

It is also as a consequence of the dissolution of the Oedipus complex that the superego is established and the individual's basic mental structure is largely determined. The child attempts to resolve his ambivalence toward the father by internalizing him and making him a part of himself. The father is set up in intrapsychic reality both as a figure who acts as a conscience and as a figure with which to identify.

In 1923 Freud called this internal figure the superego, but he had described such a figure in the internal world before. In *Mourning and Melancholia* (1917) he had shown that the self-reproaches of the melancholic are, in fact, mutual reproaches between the self and an internalized father. Furthermore, the melancholic identifies with this internal figure—"the shadow of the object fell upon the ego."[4] But at that time Freud believed such internalizations and identifications to be the domain of pathology. He later came to the conclusion that this process is part of normal development. The pathology of the melancholic's inner state lies in the excessive hatred in his ambivalence. The superego, as Freud described it in his later work, has three functions: self-observation and criticism, punishment, and setting up ideal goals. That last aspect of the superego is derived from what Freud had earlier described as "the ego ideal." The origin of the ego ideal is narcissistic: "What he projects before him as his ideal is the substitute for the lost narcissism of his childhood in which he was his own ideal."[5] In "The Ego and the Id,"[6] Freud considers the ego ideal indistinguishable from the superego, attributing ego ideal functions also to the superego. The narcissistic aim of being loved and approved of by one's own self becomes merged with the desire to be loved and approved of by the ideal internal parent, the superego. The ego may submit to the superego's demands, both because of fear of punishment and the need to be loved. Mother, as well as father, enters into the final composition of the superego.

[4] "Mourning and Melancholia," *SE* XIV, p. 249.
[5] "On Narcissim: An Introduction," *SE* XIV, p. 94.
[6] *SE* XIX.

His concepts of the superego and of the duality of life and death instincts enabled Freud to formulate the structural theory of the mind. He describes the mind as consisting of three structures. The id is the instinctual endowment. It functions on the pleasure-pain principle. That is, its only aim is to avoid pain and to seek pleasure. It takes no account of reality and deals with frustration by omnipotent hallucinatory wish-fulfilment. Out of this id, through contact with reality, evolves the ego which mediates between the id and reality; it develops a reality principle. It is, to begin with, an outer crust of the id; it is the perceptual apparatus, and it also controls the motor functions. It painfully learns the reality of frustrations, seeks to assess reality, and to find real means of satisfaction. It is also a psychic structure, being the organ of perception of inner states. When the superego is formed the ego has to mediate not only between the id and reality but also between the id and the superego. The ego has to cope not only with external but also with internal reality.

The underlying idea in psychoanalytical thinking is that we have to deal with psychic reality and psychic conflict as well as with the external world, and Freud continually investigated the roots of this inner conflict. At first he believed the sexual instincts to be in conflict with reality and self-preservation: that is, with what he called ego instincts, aimed at self-preservation. But as his work progressed, he found that this hypothesis did not cover clinical facts. In particular, repetition compulsion —the need, characteristic of neurotics, to repeat over and over again painful and traumatic experiences—did not seem explicable in terms of a conflict between the pleasure principle and reality. Sadism and masochism, important components in the neurotic makeup, were also difficult to account for. In 1920, in "Beyond the Pleasure Principle,"[7]

[7] *SE* XVIII.

he propounded another hypothesis—that of the duality
between life and death instincts. The libido, far from
being in conflict with the life instinct, is part of it and is
its sexual expression. Opposing it is the death instinct,
which derives from the biological need of the organism
to return to its prior state, ultimately to the inorganic.
Its psychical counterpart is a longing for a return to a
state of no pain—the nirvana principle. But the organism
feels threatened by the death instinct and deflects it outward. (As Freud had emphasized before, an instinct can
change its aim and its direction.) When it is deflected
outward toward an object, the death instinct is converted
into aggression: "I shall not die, you will." Instead of
dying, killing. To begin with, Freud himself treated this
hypothesis as a biological-philosophical speculation, but
as his work developed he saw the manifestation of the
death instinct in aggression as of fundamental importance. He originally considered aggression as a self-
preservative ego instinct mobilized by frustration, but he
became increasingly convinced of the existence of a
fundamental innate destructive drive. The deflection of
the death instinct, as basic as the life instinct and the
libido, could account for the importance of aggression in
psychic life. The fundamental conflict, between Eros—
life, including sexuality—and Thanatos—self-destruction
and destruction—is the deepest source of ambivalence, anxiety, and guilt. But although the two basic
instincts are in conflict, they also fuse. When in this
fusion the death instinct predominates, it gives rise to
sadism and masochism; when the life instinct predominates, aggression is at the service of the life forces and
becomes ego-syntonic: that is, it is at the service of the
ego.

Freud's definitive description of the id, the ego, and
the superego takes into account his new instinct theory.
The aggression, intolerable to the ego, is made over to the

superego—hence its savage character. Originally, Freud thought that infantile sexuality gave rise to guilt feelings, but after 1920 he came to think that aggression was the prime source of guilt. He says, "it is after all only the aggressiveness which is transformed into a sense of guilt by being suppressed and made over to the superego. I am convinced that many processes will admit of a simpler and clearer explanation if the findings of psycho-analysis with regard to the derivation of the sense of guilt are restricted to the aggressive instincts."[8] It is the death instinct which accounts for the "fatal inevitability of the sense of guilt."[9] He describes the superego of the melancholic as "a pure culture of the death instinct."[10]

Freud's views on anxiety were also influenced by his new ideas on the duality of instincts and the structure of the mind. Originally, Freud thought that anxiety was a direct biological conversion of the libido that is frustrated or blocked by repression; he imagined it as bearing the same relation to libido as vinegar bears to wine. But the ample clinical evidence soon convinced him of the reverse. It is not repression that causes anxiety but, on the contrary, anxiety that necessitates repression. But if so, what is the source of anxiety? At the time when the Oedipus complex is active, the leading anxiety, according to Freud, is castration anxiety. The little boy phantasizes and fears that as a punishment for his sexual wishes his father will castrate him. The discovery of the female genital reinforces this anxiety. The woman's lack of a penis is seen by the child as a confirmation that castration does happen. It is the castration anxiety that is the main factor in the resolution of the Oedipus complex and it is a castration anxiety which expresses itself sym-

8 "Civilization and Its Discontents," SE XXI, p. 138.
9 Ibid, p. 132.
10 "The Ego and the Id," SE XIX, p. 53.

bolically in manifold fears, including the fear of death. In 1926, in "Inhibitions, Symptoms and Anxiety"[11] Freud gives a more comprehensive account of anxiety. Reality fear is a response to an external danger. Anxiety, which has its prototype in the birth trauma, is a response to helplessness in the face of internal needs and impulses, and is reawakened at different stages of development by different danger situations. He describes four such basic threats, belonging to different phases: the loss of the object, castration fear, superego anxiety, and the loss of the love of the object. In the case of the loss of the object or its love and in the case of castration, the fear is of being overwhelmed by instinctual demands, which arise out of the life and death instincts and have no possibility of discharge. In the case of the superego anxiety it is the fear of being helpless in the face of superego attacks. Freud distinguishes between "traumatic anxiety," in which the ego is overwhelmed, and "signal anxiety," which warns that a danger of traumatic anxiety threatens. In relation to realistic fear, which is a signal that a real danger is threatening, the ego can take realistic action. When the signal anxiety of a threatening internal danger appears, the ego evolves psychical mechanisms of defense.

Freud first discovered repression in his study of hysteria and described it as a defense, but in his study of obsessional neurosis he found that there are other mechanisms of defense as well. In one of these, for instance, the affect is separated from the idea, so that in the obsessional person (as distinct from the hysteric) the anxiety-producing idea may remain in consciousness but the affect is repressed. As psychoanalytical knowledge progressed, more mechanisms of defense were discovered and described.

[11] *SE* XX.

Four of them became of particular importance to the work of Melanie Klein, and I shall briefly describe them. They are: projection, introjection, identification, and splitting. Projection and introjection have their origin in the pure pleasure ego as it develops from the id and continues under the sway of the pleasure-pain principle: "the original pleasure ego wants to introject into itself everything that is good and to eject from itself everything that is bad."[12]

Projection as a mechanism of defense is characteristic of paranoia. The subject disowns his own impulses and attributes them to his object. "I do not hate him—he hates me." Introjection, a term first used by Ferenczi, is the opposite of projection. Based on the earliest oral impulse to eat the object, it has a mental counterpart: introjecting the object's characteristics. Freud first described it in relation to melancholia; later he came to the conclusion that it is part of normal development and that the ego cannot give up its object without introjecting it. In "The Ego and the Id," he says that the ego is "a precipitate of abandoned object cathexes."[13] Though introjection is rooted in oral mechanism and therefore must be active from the beginning, Freud considers that the introjections at the time of the Oedipus complex are so massive and dynamic that earlier introjections do not have the same influence or importance.

Freud discovered identification before introjection and sometimes they are not clearly differentiated. He describes various kinds of identification. One is identification of the self with the object as the model. The subject assimilates the characteristics of the object; thus identification can be a defense against the loss of the object or rivalry with it. Such an identification with the parents

[12] "Negation," *SE* XIX, p. 237.
[13] *SE* XIX, p. 29.

is part of the resolution of the Oedipus complex. Another type of identification is the narcissistic object choice. Here it is the subject that is the model and one's own characteristics are sought in the object. Identifications may be pre-Oedipal or Oedipal. As Freud described identification before introjection it is unclear whether he considers pre-Oedipal identifications to be based on introjection or to be independent of it, but characteristic of the Oedipus complex is an introjective identification with the parents.

Splitting of the ego is a mechanism Freud observed in cases of fetishism and in psychosis. Originally he applied it solely to disturbances in relation to reality. The ego splits itself so that there is one part, the normal ego, which takes account of reality, and another which, under the influence of the instincts, detaches itself from reality. But in his very last papers[14] he comments that the use of any mechanism of defense necessitates some splitting of the ego and that, therefore, an excessive use of defenses is always weakening to the ego.

Prominent among the psychoanalysts who augmented in important ways the body of psychoanalytic knowledge was Karl Abraham, who became a major influence on Melanie Klein. He contributed to all aspects of psychoanalytical theory but his major and most original contribution lies in the field of the pre-genital phases of development.[15] He subdivided both the oral and the anal phases. He divided the oral phase into a first oral sucking stage and a second oral sadistic one. The first is pre-ambivalent: the infant's aim is to suck, but there is

[14] "An Outline of Psycho-Analysis," *SE* XXIII, pp. 202–204; "Splitting of the Ego in the Process of Defence," ibid., pp. 275–278.
[15] K. Abraham, "A Short Study of the Development of the Libido, Viewed in the Light of Mental Disorders" (1924), in *Selected Papers of Karl Abraham*, pp. 418–501.

neither love nor hate. In the second stage the infant relates to the breast in an ambivalent way and wishes to bite it and to devour it cannibalistically. The first anal stage is expulsive and sadistic; the sadism of the second oral phase continues, and the devoured object, turned into feces, is expelled. The second anal stage is retentive. In that stage concern for the object appears, and though the object—the stool—is still controlled sadistically, there is also a wish to preserve it. The object in its pre-genital phase is a part object, a term introduced by Abraham to designate the relation to anatomical parts of the parents, such as the breast or the penis, in contradistinction to parents as people. Freud described some relations to part objects, for instance, the infant's original desire for the breast. He also spoke of regressing to a part-object relationship—for example, the woman regressing from a desire for the man to a desire for the penis, which is a part object—but he did not attach much importance to such pre-genital fixations. Abraham, on the contrary, studied in great detail the oral and anal relationship to part objects such as the part-object breast and its transformation into the part-object stool. He was the first to describe the loss of an internal object in this process, expelling the stool being experienced as losing an internal object. His concern with the oral stages of development led him also to attach more importance than Freud did to the ambivalent relation of the infant to the mother. In particular, he found that in melancholia the hatred of the mother plays an essential role.

These subdivisions are not a mere academic exercise. Abraham based them on his clinical work, and he was able to demonstrate that the fixation point of the manic-depressive illnesses lies in the second oral and first anal phases, and that of obsessional neuroses in the second anal phase. He was able to analyze effectively patients suffering from manic-depressive psychosis as well as obsessional neurotics, and this work enabled him to study the interrelation between depression, mania, and obsessional neurosis, as well as to extend our knowledge into the oral and anal phases of development.

Melanie Klein started her work just before 1920, when psychoanalysis was at one of its turning points and Freud's new ideas were giving a stimulus to new approaches. Developing his thought in the direction taken by Abraham, she brought to psychoanalysis new and inspiring ideas and perspectives. But her work also aroused strong opposition, and gave rise to controversies which are still active.

Before introducing Melanie Klein's work, it may be important to say something about the psychoanalytic technique since, in psychoanalysis, theory and technique are intimately interrelated.

Starting with the simple application of hypnosis, Freud developed the psychoanalytical technique. The essentials of the psychoanalytic setting and technique as devised by Freud could be described briefly as follows. The analyst offers the patient a regular hour every weekday. He invites him to lie down on the couch and tell his thoughts as freely as he can: that is, to free-associate. The analyst is receptive to the patient's communications and refrains from any personal reaction such as criticism, approval, conveying or expressing his feelings. In such a setting, of which the analyst's neutrality is an essential ingredient, the patient can associate more freely than in any other situation, and gradually his unconscious conflicts express themselves in a way that the analyst can perceive; he can then communicate to the patient the hidden meaning of his associations—that is, interpret. This psychoanalytical process of free associations and interpretation is, however, resisted by the patient. Whatever defenses he originally developed against the pain caused by the conflict are mobilized again as resistance to insight and that resistance has also to be understood and analyzed. The patient comes originally because of his need, and cooperates by free-associating and trying to understand and overcome his own resistance. In the analytic situation the patient not only becomes aware of his infantile wishes and conflicts, he relives them. He transfers on to the analyst the impulses, expectations, and phantasies he had in the past in relation to his significant objects—parents, siblings, et al. This transference, first considered to be a resistance to remembering the past, gradually became the pivot of the psychoanalytic treatment. It is because the patient relives old conflicts again more openly and in a new setting that he can find new, less neurotic solutions. Positive transference (love) also promotes cooperation.

Klein never departed from the basic psychoanalytical setting and technique and, indeed, in many respects her technique was particularly rigorous.

The Early Years

Melanie Klein was born in Vienna in 1882. Her father, Dr. Moriz Reizes, came from a strictly orthodox Jewish family, and as he was considered by his parents to be very bright, they decided that he should become a rabbi. They married him off to a girl he had never seen. The young man, however, rebelled against orthodoxy. In secret, he studied, acquired the German *matura,* and went to a medical school, despite his parents' opposition. He became independent of his family, but never entirely broke off with them. Indeed, when his father was a very old man and none of the other children would keep him, it was the rebel son, Dr. Reizes, who looked after him until his death. When he became independent, Dr. Reizes divorced his first wife and at the age of over forty fell deeply in love and married Libusa Deutsch, then aged twenty-five, to whom he remained devoted. There were four children of this marriage, the youngest of whom was Melanie. Dr. Reizes was not very successful as a doctor and to help make ends meet his wife opened a shop of exotic plants and animals. When Melanie was five, however, he inherited some money, which enabled him to buy a dental practice in which he was much more successful. Melanie remembered clearly how delighted she was by the new and bigger apartment and the easier circumstances. Her relation to her father was not very close. He was well over fifty when she was born and had little patience with the small child. He also frequently and overtly expressed his preference for his eldest daughter, which Melanie naturally deeply resented. On the other hand, she was tremendously impressed and stimulated by her father's intellectual achievements. For instance, he taught himself ten European languages. He was also widely read and, as Melanie grew older, was always ready to answer her many questions. He died when she was eighteen.

She had a far closer relation with her mother, whom she remembered as a woman much younger than her father, very beautiful, warmhearted, courageous, and enterprising. Not only did she keep a shop—an unusual thing for a doctor's wife to do in those days—but later, when Melanie was finishing school and her father became ailing and somewhat senile, it was her mother who supplemented the family income and kept the family together. She spent the last few years of her life in Melanie Klein's home, which was a great solace to Melanie at a generally unhappy time of her life. Libusa died in 1914. Melanie was deeply moved by the serenity and courage with which her mother approached death after a long-drawn-out illness, and often spoke of it in her old age.

Melanie's upbringing was liberal and easygoing, and

she remembered her childhood as mostly serene and happy. Religion played little part in the family life. Her father, after his rebellion, was rather anticlerical; and Melanie herself disliked the orthodox caftan-clad members of her father's family. Her mother also came from a rabbinical family, but of quite a different kind. They were enlightened, liberal and well-read in philosophy and the humanities. In contrast to her father, her mother kept some allegiance to the Jewish religion and even tried half-heartedly and unsuccessfully to introduce kosher cooking into the house. She kept the yearly fast and went to the synagogue once a year.

Melanie Klein herself was not religious. At the age of nine or ten, under the influence of a French governess to whom she was very attached, she became attracted to the Catholic religion. For a time she was tortured by the idea that she might become a Catholic, knowing the pain it would cause her parents. But apart from this youthful episode, she remained remarkably free from either religious or bitterly antireligious feelings. She was an atheist and, detesting hypocrisy, she made quite certain that no religious service would be held at her funeral for social or conventional reasons. She also opposed the teaching of religion by nonbelieving parents "for the child's own good." She firmly held that one must never teach children beliefs one does not hold oneself. On the other hand, she was very aware of her Jewish roots, liked some of the Jewish traditions, and had little respect for those who denied their Jewishness.

Melanie's eldest sibling, Emily, was six years older than she; Emmanuel, the only brother, five years older; and Sidonie about four years older. She was deeply marked by her relation to Sidonie and Emmanuel, both of whom died tragically young. She saw little of Sidonie, who suffered from scrofula and spent a good deal of her childhood in a hospital, but Melanie remembered vividly the last months of Sidonie's life, which she spent at home. Melanie, the youngest, was at that time often teased by the two eldest children and Sidonie took her under her wing. She taught her to read and to write. The little girl of eight was very aware of her approaching death and she told Melanie that she wanted to pass on to her all she knew before dying. She died at the age of nine, when Melanie was about five. She had a longer-lasting relation with her brother, Emmanuel, and she considered it as being most formative for her. An exceptionally talented young man, who played the piano and wrote essays and poetry, he began to study medicine but abandoned it because of ill health. When Melanie was nine or ten he saw a poem of hers which he liked, and from then on they developed a close friendship which lasted until his death in his mid-twenties. When she was fourteen, Melanie decided that she wanted to go to the university and study medicine. To do that she had to move from the *lyceum,* which gave only a superficial education, to the *gymnasium,* which prepared for the *matura* and the university. It was her brother who coached her in the Greek and Latin needed to pass her entrance examination. As she grew a little older, he introduced her to his circle of friends, a very lively intellectual group in which Melanie blossomed. He was somewhat rebellious and fought a great deal with his father. It says something for the intellectual atmosphere of the house that the worst row which Melanie remembered between her father and her brother had to do with their disagreement on the relative merits of Goethe and Schiller, her father screaming with fury that Goethe was a mountebank with scientific pretensions.

Emmanuel suffered from a rheumatic heart condition and he, like Sidonie, was aware of impending death. He once wrote to Melanie that he wished fate would give her as many happy years as the days it was going to deprive him of. He had a great confidence in her talents and always predicted a great future for her. She, on her side, admired him deeply. When he died suddenly, while abroad, Melanie, by then married and living in Slovakia, traveled back to Vienna, though pregnant, and devoted herself to the task of getting his poems and essays published. The project did not succeed: first, because the publishing firm which had accepted them for publication went bankrupt, and later, because of the outbreak of war.

The deaths of these two siblings, especially, perhaps, that of Emmanuel, contributed not a little to the lasting streak of depression which was part of Melanie's personality. At the same time, they both stimulated her intellectual interests and gave her a feeling of having almost a duty to seek development and achievement.

It was through her brother that Melanie had met her future husband, Arthur Stephen Klein. The fact that he was her brother's friend must have added to the young man's glamour. She was also at that time overimpressed by intellectual achievement and was dazzled by Klein's intellect. Her engagement to him at the age of nineteen interfered with her plans to study medicine, as her future husband, an engineer, would have to travel to various factories and could not remain in Vienna. She spent the two years of her engagement studying humanities at Vienna University. All her life she regretted not having studied medicine, believing that if she had had a medical degree her views would have been listened to with more respect. This feeling became particularly acute at the time of her controversy with Edward Glover, a prominent British psychoanalyst. Glover originally supported her work with children and considered it to be a major contribution to psychoanalysis, but when she developed her theories about the origin of psychosis, he took great objection to the fact that a lay person with no medical knowledge should talk at all about psychosis.

Melanie married at the age of twenty-one, and for several years lived with her husband in small towns, first in Slovakia then in Silesia. It was an unhappy time. She missed the intellectual company and stimulation she had enjoyed in Vienna, and the marriage was from the beginning full of problems. She turned to reading and learning languages, but her only true happiness was with her two children, Melitta, born in 1904, and Hans, born in 1907.

Her life changed considerably when in 1910 her husband at last found work in Budapest. There she found the intellectual companionship she wanted and, even more important, it was there that she first encountered Freud's work. In Vienna, although she moved in literary and artistic circles, she had never heard of Freud. Later she greatly regretted the opportunities she had missed. Living in the same town, she might have sought to meet him, and even to study with him. In Budapest, she came across Freud's popularizing book. *On Dreams* (1901).[1] Thus began her lifelong interest in psychoanalysis. To study psychoanalysis, practice it, contribute to it, became the ruling passion of her life. She sought analysis with Ferenczi, and with his encouragement started to analyze children. In 1917 she was introduced to Freud at a meeting between the Austrian and Hungarian Societies. She read her first paper, "The Development of a Child,"[2] to the Hungarian Society in 1919, and on the strength of that paper became a member of the Budapest Society. She stayed in Budapest until 1919, when her third child, Eric, was five years old. She then separated from her husband, who went to work in Sweden, while she spent a year with

[1] *SE* V.
[2] Part I of "The Development of a Child" (1921), *Writings* I.

her parents-in-law in Slovakia. This separation was a prelude to the divorce which occurred in 1922. In 1920, at a psychoanalytic congress in The Hague, Melanie Klein had met Karl Abraham and was deeply impressed by him. He himself spoke encouragingly of her work in child analysis, which prompted her in 1921 to move to Berlin. There, she established a psychoanalytical practice with adults as well as children. She was not satisfied with the results of her analysis with Ferenczi and in 1924 she persuaded Abraham to take her on as a patient. Abraham was generally averse to analyzing colleagues resident in Berlin, but he was convinced of the importance and the potential of her contribution to psychoanalysis. At the First Congress of German Analysts in 1924, in summing up Mrs. Klein's paper on the Erna case,[3] he said: "The future of psycho-analysis lies in play techniques." He agreed to make an exception and undertook to analyze her. This analysis was abruptly interrupted by Abraham's death only fourteen months later.

Melanie Klein's relation to her two analysts was very different. She felt grateful to Ferenczi for the encouragement he gave to her work and she also felt that she derived from his analysis a conviction about the importance of unconscious dynamics. But Ferenczi did not analyze the negative transference (hostile feelings toward the analyst), and she felt that this analysis did not give her any lasting insight. Also, Ferenczi gradually abandoned the analytic technique and devised "active techniques." He gave up the role of the analyst as a neutral interpreter and actively encouraged, reassured, or directed the patient. This eventually led to a split with Freud. Klein, from the start, opposed those developments as being out of keeping with psychoanalytical principles and she grieved for Ferenczi. For Abraham she had unmitigated

[3] *Writings* II, pp. 35–57.

gratitude and admiration. The fourteen months' analysis she had with him gave her, she thought, a true understanding of psychoanalysis. His premature death was one of the great losses of her life. But she was determined to continue his work. She started an intense and regular self-analysis which she carried on for many years. Although she took from Ferenczi the concept of introjection, Abraham's work, particularly on melancholia, was the more important influence. She considered herself his pupil and her work a contribution and development of Freud's and Abraham's.

After Abraham's death, life in Berlin became difficult for Melanie Klein. Not only was the loss of Abraham and the interruption of her analysis a deep grief, but also, lacking his support, she found her work in Berlin under constant attack. Anna Freud had started work with children at about the same time as Melanie Klein, but their approach was different and there was considerable controversy and conflict between the two. The Berlin Society in the main followed Anna Freud and considered Mrs. Klein's work "unorthodox." In 1925 Klein met Ernest Jones at a conference in Salzburg, where she gave her first paper on the technique of child analysis, a paper which was very controversial.[4] Jones was impressed by this paper and concurred with Abraham's statement that the future of psychoanalysis rested with child analysis. Stimulated by the opinion of Alix Strachey, who had been in analysis with Abraham in Berlin, and of Joan Riviere, who from the beginning took an interest in Melanie Klein's work, Jones invited Klein to give some lectures on child analysis in England. So in 1925, in the house of Dr. Adrian Stephen, she gave six lectures which formed the basis of the initial part of *The Psycho-Analysis of Children*, her

[4] Published in 1926 under the title "The Psychological Principles of Early Analysis," *Writings* I, pp. 128–38.

first book. The three weeks in which she gave these lectures she considered one of the happiest times of her life.

In 1927 Melanie Klein established herself in England, where she was to remain until she died. This was a decision that she never regretted. Though she had difficulties and there were controversies in the British Psychoanalytic Society, unavoidable in view of the revolutionary nature of her work, she felt that by and large she had had a better reception and more support in the British Society than she would have found anywhere else. She also became deeply attached to England as the country of her adoption. She brought with her her youngest son, Eric, then thirteen, and a few years later Melitta, who had married Dr. Walter Schmideberg, also came to London. Both were doctors and practicing psychoanalysts. Her eldest son, Hans, following his father's footsteps, became an engineer and remained in Berlin.

The Play Technique

iii

When Melanie Klein arrived in London in 1927, her technique of child analysis, which she called play analysis, was fully worked out.

To appreciate how revolutionary this technique was, we have to say something about the beginning of psychoanalysis of children. As is almost always the case in psychoanalytical discoveries, the first steps were taken by Freud. He assumed, from the analysis of adults, that adult neurosis was rooted in a childhood neurosis existing at the time of the Oedipus complex. "From the History of an Infantile Neurosis" (1918),[1] which describes the case of the man who came to be known as the Wolf Man, shows most clearly how in analyzing the patient's adult neurosis Freud unearthed the structure of an infantile

[1] SE XVII, pp. 7–122.

neurosis from which the patient suffered in prelatency. But though he observed his own children and encouraged his pupils to gather what observations they could, there was no systematic study of child neurosis, with one exception. In 1909 Freud published the case history of Little Hans.[2] Hans was a little boy of five, who suffered from an agoraphobia related to his fear of being bitten by a horse in the street. Encouraged by Freud and under Freud's supervision, the boy's own father analyzed him and managed to uncover his Oedipus complex, both positive and negative, with the result that Hans's neurosis abated. This case history directly confirmed Freud's hypotheses about childhood neurosis, and it also showed that children could be analyzed and that this neurosis might possibly be resolved at its inception. At the time of publication, Freud thought that only the father himself could undertake such an analysis, but subsequently he altered this view. In later papers, notably in the one describing the Wolf Man, where he discusses the possible advantages of psychoanalyzing children, he makes no such restrictions.

Despite this hopeful and brilliant beginning, child analysis did not thrive. There were probably unconscious factors of resistance at play. All their psychoanalytical knowledge notwithstanding, analysts seemed wary of disturbing "childhood innocence." Melanie Klein told me that when she first produced child material in the Berlin Society there was indignation, not only at her views about children's aggression but also at her talking to children about sexuality in such a direct manner. And this was more than ten years after the publication of Little Hans.

But there were also technical difficulties. How to apply a psychoanalytic technique to children? Adults seek

---

[2] "Analysis of a Phobia in a Five-Year-Old Boy," *SE* X, pp. 5–149.

analysis because of their awareness of illness. Most analysts before Melanie Klein considered that children do not have a sense of illness and need for help, and that it was therefore impossible to expect their cooperation. Also one could not make a child lie still on the couch and free-associate. And children, it was thought, still attached to their parents, would not develop a transference.

Klein's stroke of genius lay in noticing that the child's natural mode of expressing himself was play, and that play could therefore be used as a means of communication with the child. Play for the child is not "just play." It is also work. It is not only a way of exploring and mastering the external world but also, through expressing and working through phantasies, a means of exploring and mastering anxieties. In his play the child dramatizes his phantasies, and in doing so elaborates and works through his conflicts.

Freud treated play as a symptomatic act and quite naturally included it in the analysis. He noticed, for instance, how Dora played with her reticule and interpreted the meaning of this play.[3] In *The Psychopathology of Everyday Life* (1901)[4] he described a consultation with a young adolescent whom he could not get to speak about his conflicts; but he noticed that the boy was making a figure out of a bread pellet. Freud used that symptomatic act, to which he drew the boy's attention, as a first communication about the boy's sexual problems. Later on the boy chopped off the breadman's head, which Freud again used in his explanations. But neither Freud nor those who before or at the same time as Klein tried to analyze children, had realized the full importance of play to the child, or thought of using it as the major route of access to the child's unconscious.

[3] "Fragment of an Analysis of a Case of Hysteria" (1905), *SE* XII, pp. 76–79.
[4] *SE* VI, p. 198.

Melanie Klein, giving full weight to the role of play, concluded that, given the right conditions, the child's free play, as well as whatever verbal communications he is capable of, could serve a purpose similar to that of free associations in adults.

> In their play, children represent symbolically phantasies, wishes and experiences. Here they are employing the same language, the same archaic, philogenetically acquired mode of expression as we are familiar with from dreams. We can only fully understand it if we approach it by the method Freud has evolved for unravelling dreams. Symbolism is only a part of it; if we want rightly to comprehend children's play in connection with their whole behaviour during the analytic hour we must take into account not only the symbolism which often appears so clearly in their games but also all the means of representation and the mechanisms employed in dreamwork, and we must bear in mind the necessity of examining the whole nexus of phenomena.[5]

In the chapter on "Technique of Early Analysis" in *The Psycho-Analysis of Children,* she gives the following simple example to illustrate the symbolism of the child's play and her technique in analyzing it. Peter, an anxious, plaintive, inhibited little boy of three and a half, got on badly with other children, particularly with his brother, and was on occasion sneering and aggressive.

> At the very beginning of his first session Peter took the toy carriages and cars and put them first one behind the other and then side by side, and alternated this arrangement several times. In between he took two horse-drawn carriages and bumped one into another, so that the horses' feet knocked together, and said: "I've got a new little brother called Fritz." I asked him what the carriages were doing. He answered: "That's not nice," and stopped bumping them together at once, but started again quite soon. Then he knocked two toy horses together in the same way. Upon which I said:

[5] *Writings* I, p. 134.

"Look here, the horses are two people bumping together." At first he said: "No, that's not nice," but then,
"Yes, that's two people bumping together," and added:
"The horses have bumped together too, and now they're
going to sleep." Then he covered them up with bricks
and said: "Now they're quite dead; I've buried them."[6]

In the first session she only drew his attention to the
fact that his toys symbolized people. In the next session
he put two swings side by side and, showing Mrs. Klein
the inner and longish part that hung down and swung,
he said, "Look how it dangles and bumps." At that point
Mrs. Klein interpreted that the two swings were Daddy
and Mummy bumping their "thingummies" (his word
for genitals) together. The child first objected, repeated
"No, that isn't nice," but went on with the game, saying,
"That's how they bumped their thingummies together,"
and immediately afterward spoke again about his little
brother. In the first session the knocking together of the
two carriages and horses had also been followed by his
remarking that he had got a new little brother, so Mrs.
Klein interpreted the child's thought that when Daddy
and Mummy bumped their thingummies together that
led to his little brother being born. The child's playing
developed in subsequent sessions, indicating his own
wish to take part in the intercourse. Later, in his symbolic play, and in more direct reactions such as suddenly
having to urinate or to defecate, he expressed his Oedipal conflicts and his conflicts around his bisexuality. The
death wishes to his parents and brother, indicated already in the first session by his knocking toys down in a
rage and saying, "They're dead," became increasingly
clear and could be interpreted.

Realizing the significance of play in childhood, Melanie
Klein also drew attention to inhibition of play as a very

6 *Writings* II, p. 17.

important symptom, indicating an inhibition of phantasy life and of general development. For some children, hampered in their capacity to play, only psychoanalytic treatment relieves the inhibition. In the treatment itself, free play can be inhibited just like free association. This may manifest itself either by a complete stoppage of play or by rigid, unimaginative repetitiveness. Like resistance to free association in the analysis of adults, such inhibitions of free play can be resolved when the underlying anxiety is lessened by interpretation.

> The play which was interrupted, owing to the setting up of resistances, is resumed; it alters, expands and expresses deeper strata of the mind; the contact between the child and the analyst is re-established. The pleasure in play, which visibly ensues after an interpretation has been given, is also due to the fact that the expenditure necessitated by a repression is no longer required after an interpretation.[7]

These insights about the significance of children's play are today commonplace, but at the time they opened a whole new area in the understanding of children.

Melanie Klein herself gave a short account of her technique in a paper presented in 1946 to the British Psychological Society.[8] The first child she attempted to analyze was a five-year-old boy whom she called Fritz. She analyzed him in 1920 for a few months, in his own home and with his own toys. The aim she set herself in this first analysis was to analyze a child with the same objective in view as she would have in the analysis of an adult; that is, to bring unconscious conflict into consciousness, using the same rules in interpreting the material as she would in the analysis of an adult, paying

7 *Writings* I, p. 134.
8 "The Psycho-Analytic Play Technique: Its History and Significance" (1955), *Writings* III, pp. 122–40.

particular attention to the transference, negative as well as positive. The child was often very anxious and sometimes Klein's interpretations mobilized the anxiety. She tried to resolve it by interpreting its roots. At one point she herself became anxious and uncertain because of the intensity of the child's anxiety, but she was then encouraged by Abraham to continue with her chosen technique. And indeed, after interpretations, the child's anxiety abated, and despite the shortness of the analysis, the therapeutic results seemed to have been good.

Her next important step, in 1923, was the analysis of the little girl, Rita, aged two and three-quarters, a severely disturbed child with *pavor nocturnus* (night terrors).[9] This analysis she also began in the child's own nursery in the watchful and ambivalent presence of the child's aunt and mother. In the first session the child was too anxious to stay with Mrs. Klein in the nursery and she ran out into the garden. Mrs. Klein then directly interpreted negative transference, telling Rita that she was afraid of what Mrs. Klein might do to her, and connecting this fear with the child's *pavor nocturnus*. After these interpretations, the child returned quietly to the nursery and continued playing with Mrs. Klein. However, she soon came to the conclusion that she could not analyze the child at home and transferred the analysis to her consulting room. This was an important step. She realized then that the analysis of a child, like that of an adult, needs a proper psychoanalytical setting, away from its home and family.

Following that experience, she analyzed another little girl,[10] and it is in this analysis that she developed the technique of using special toys for the child. She gave

[9] *Writings* II, pp. 3–4, 6, 8.
[10] "The Psycho-Analytic Play Technique" (1955), *Writings* III, p. 125.

the little girl a box of toys to be used only by her in the analytical sessions.

In 1923 her principles of child analysis and her technique were fully established. She provided the child with an appropriate psychoanalytical setting: that is, the child had his or her sessions at strictly defined times—fifty minutes, five times a week. The room was specially adapted for the child. It would contain only simple and sturdy furniture, a small table and chair for the child, a chair for the analyst, a small couch. The floor and the walls would be washable. Each child would have its own box of toys, used only for the treatment. The toys were carefully chosen. There were little houses, little men and women, preferably in two sizes, farm and wild animals, bricks, balls, maybe marbles, also play material such as scissors, string, pencils, paper, Plasticine. Besides that, the room would have water, since in some phases of the analyses of many children water plays a very important role. The choice of the toys is important since the child's free play functions like free association in the analysis of the adult. The toys should not dictate playing. As in the analysis of adults, the analyst must not suggest the theme of the associations, so the toys must not suggest the theme of the play. There should be no toys which have their own special meaning, such as toy telephones, or games which impose rules, such as draughts; the human figures are in two sizes to facilitate the representation of child and adult roles, but they are quite unspecific. They should have no uniforms or special dress, nor any indication of occupation or role which would suggest a particular kind of play. The toys are very small—this was Klein's intuitive choice. Very small toys seem to lend themselves particularly to play analysis, possibly because the smallness makes them specially appropriate to represent the inner world. Donald Winnicott, introducing Mrs.

Klein's paper on play technique in the British Psychological Society, said that he considered her introduction of these tiny toys as the most significant advance in child analysis. With them the child is free to express himself and make such use of them as is most appropriate to his phantasy.

Melanie Klein held that the child's play expresses its preoccupations, conflicts, and phantasies, and her technique consisted in analyzing the play exactly as one analyzes dreams and free associations, interpreting phantasies, conflicts, and defenses. The child's drawings and his associations to them are often particularly instructive.

From the time of the analysis of Little Hans until 1919 only Hug Helmuth had attempted to analyze children. Anna Freud, in about the same years as Melanie Klein, started developing a child technique based on that of Hug Helmuth. The differences between the approaches of Anna Freud and Melanie Klein were considerable, and the controversy between them came to a head at the Symposium of Child Analysis in 1927. Miss Freud, like Hug Helmuth, contended that the child developed no transference neurosis. The general theory of the transference is that the patient transfers on to the analyst feelings and phantasies belonging to his relationship with the parents in the past. Eventually the neurotic conflict which has evolved in the relation to the parents manifests itself in the transference neurosis. According to Miss Freud, this transference could not occur when the child was still dependent on the parents: "The old edition is not yet exhausted."[11] She also considered that the analysis of a child should be educative as well as analytical in order to strengthen its superego and she thought negative transference was to be avoided. Valuable work

[11] A. Freud, *The Psycho-Analytical Treatment of Children,* p. 34.

with children was done only in positive transference.

Melanie Klein found that though the children do not often have "a sense of illness" in the adult sense, they suffer from acute anxieties and are at least as aware as an adult of need for help. In contrast to Miss Freud, she considered that because of their anxiety and general dependence children develop a transference to the analyst early and strongly. The fact that they are still dependent on their parents does not preclude the development of the transference, since it is not the relationship to the real parents that is transferred on to the analyst but the relationship to the internal phantasy figure—the parental imago. From the beginning she paid particular attention to the child's inner world and the nature of the inner figures transferred on to the analyst. The internal parents are often split into ideal and very bad figures. The child defends itself against its ambivalence toward its parents by such splitting, and now the ideal, now the persecutory aspect of the parents is attributed to the analyst. Klein felt that educational methods had no place in psychoanalysis and interfered in the development of the psychoanalytical process. She says that "a true *analytic* situation can be brought about only by *analytic* means,"[12] and if one employs nonanalytical means like educative methods or efforts to obtain a positive transference, then naturally an ânalytical situation would not develop. She also thought that if the analyst sought at all costs to obtain a positive transference, then the child would shift all its split-off hostile feelings on to his parents or other people in his environment. In that situation, the child's other relationships would suffer and his essential conflict, his fear of a persecutory superego, would remain unanalyzed.

Those technical differences were of course linked with

[12] "Symposium on Child Analysis" (1927), *Writings* I, p. 143.

differences in theoretical approach. According to Freud, the superego is formed on the dissolution of the Oedipus complex. Before that the child fears the authority of the real parents. The introjection of the parents' prohibitions and the formation of an internal authority—the superego —heralds the approach of latency. The young child's superego was supposed to be inexistent or weak. This theoretical concept was the basis of Miss Freud's attitude and technique. Melanie Klein, on the contrary, was led to believe by her observation of children in analysis that the young child has phantasies of terrifying, punishing internal parents, constituting, in fact, a particularly savage superego with which the child's ego cannot cope. She thought, therefore, that in the analysis of children, as in that of adults, it is the analysis of the superego in the transference, aimed at diminishing its severity, that allows a strengthening and a better development of the ego. The analysis of the internal figures composing the superego, the resolution of anxiety and guilt connected with those figures, was the aim of her approach.

In the development of psychoanalysis there is an intimate relation between theory and technique. It was the technique of hypnosis that enabled Freud to discover the unconscious process. His thinking on this unconscious process in turn led him to the technique of free association, and the technique of free association gave him the material for the formulation of his theoretical views. Mrs. Klein approached the psychoanalysis of children armed with Freud's theories and technique. Her play technique was devised as a method of communication with the child which allowed her to adhere to psychoanalytical principles. It gave her access to the unconscious of the child, and this in turn enabled her to make discoveries which altered her theoretical views on child sexuality and the development of the psychic apparatus.

Whereas Freud deduced the psychology of the child from the psychoanalysis of adults—with the single exception of Little Hans—she studied infantile conflicts and structure directly in the child.

IV

Mrs. Klein's first discoveries related to the Oedipus complex. Very early in her work with children she had observed that the Oedipus complex, which it was believed at the time would not start before the age of four and would reach its acme at about the age of six, was well in evidence in children much younger. For instance in Rita, aged two and three-quarters,[1] she traced the *pavor nocturnus* from which the child suffered to her phantasies of the parental intercourse and the Oedipal attacks she made in phantasy on her mother, which in turn led to the formation of a terrifying phantasy of a mother who persecuted her in her nightmares and night terrors. Similarly, Klein observed that the superego was a much earlier—and more complicated—formation

[1] *Writings* II, pp. 3–4, 6, 8.

than was thought at the time. She found that the super-ego was not a "precipitate," coming at the end of the Oedipus complex, but was part and parcel of the Oedipus complex. Thus one could consider, for instance, the terrifying mother figure coming to punish Rita in retaliation for her attacks as an early form of the superego. She found in her investigation of children that the child's life was dominated by unconscious and sometimes conscious phantasies about the parents' sexuality. The frustrations, jealousies, and envies produced by the child's Oedipal situation lead to sadistic attacks and these in turn lead to the formation of the terrifying figures which compose the child's early superego. Moreover, Klein had discovered that the Oedipus complex itself has pre-genital forms. According to the child's stage of libidinal development, he phantasizes his parents as exchanging libidinal gratifications, such as mutual feeding and sucking at the oral stage or exchanges of urine and feces or anal penetration at the anal stage. Those phantasies give rise to real Oedipal jealousy and envy. In disturbed children in particular, pre-genital forms may dominate the picture. Take, for example, Erna,[2] a little girl of six who suffered from a severe obsessional neurosis. Her phantasies took a marked character, first oral, then anal-sadistic. For instance, at the beginning of her treatment, she put a toy man and a toy woman together. She said that they were to love one another all the time. But soon she made a third figure (a little man) run them over, kill, and roast them, and then eat them up. The little man represented herself. Many games ended in parental figures being roasted and eaten up. Her sadistic cannibalistic impulses were well in evidence. For instance, while cutting up paper she was associating that she was making mincemeat and that blood was coming out of the paper; and soon

[2] Ibid., pp. 35–57.

after she felt sick. On other occasions, she made what she called an "eye-salad," and said that she was cutting fringes out of Mrs. Klein's nose. These games symbolized her sadistic and cannibalistic phantasy attacks on her parents and, by reason of transference, on Mrs. Klein. She also played many games symbolizing the eating of her mother's breast or her father's penis, which she called something "long and golden." Her anal phantasies were equally evident. She imagined her parents' intercourse often in terms of defecating and in phantasy she used her own feces sadistically for soiling, burning, and poisoning.

Rita, Mrs. Klein's youngest patient, showed that such phantasies and fears were already active in a very small child. Rita was less than three years old when she began to exhibit overt neurotic symptoms. She was inhibited in play, oversensitive to reproach, and suffering from exaggerated guilt and anxiety. When she played with a doll she took no pleasure in it and kept repeating that the doll was not her child:

Analysis showed that she was not permitted to play at being its mother, because, among other things, the doll child stood for her little brother whom she had wanted to steal from her mother during the latter's pregnancy. The prohibition, however, did not proceed from her real mother, but from an introjected one who treated her with far more severity and cruelty than the real one had ever done. Another symptom—an obsession—which Rita developed at the age of two was a bed-time ritual which took up a lot of time. The main point of it was that she had to be tightly tucked up in the bedclothes, otherwise a "mouse, or a *Butzen*" would get in through the window and bite off her own "*Butzen*." (Rita's castration complex was manifested in a whole series of symptoms and also in her characterological development. Her play, too, clearly showed the strength of her identification with her father and her fear—arising from her castration complex—of failing in the masculine role.) Her doll had to be tucked up too, and this double ceremonial became more and more elaborate and long-drawn-out and was performed with every sign of that compulsive attitude which pervaded her whole mind. On one occasion during her analytic session she put a toy elephant on her doll's bed so as to prevent it from getting up and going into her parents' bedroom and "doing something to them or taking something away from them." The elephant was taking over the role of her internalized parents whose prohibiting influence she felt ever since, between the ages of one year and three months and two years, she had wished to take her mother's place with her father, rob her of the child inside her, and injure and castrate both parents. The meaning of the ceremonial now became clear: being tucked up in bed was to prevent her from getting up and carrying out her aggressive wishes against her parents. Since, however, she expected to be punished for those wishes by a similar attack on herself by her parents, being tucked up also served as a defence against such attacks. The attacks were to be made, for instance, by the *"Butzen"* (her father's penis), which would injure her genitals and bite off her own *"Butzen"* as a punishment for wanting to castrate him. In these games she used to punish her doll and then give way to an outburst of rage and fear, thus showing that she was playing both parts herself— that of the powers which inflict punishment and that of the punished child itself.

These games also proved that this anxiety referred not only to the child's real parents, but also, and more especially, to its excessively stern introspected parents. What we meet with here corresponds to what we call the super-ego in adults. (In my opinion the child's earliest identifications already deserve to be called "superego". . . .)[3]

Erna had phantasies of being cruelly persecuted by her mother and considered every step in her education, every frustration, and even every amusement her mother enjoyed as a persecution and punishment. She had

[3] Ibid., pp. 6–7.

frightening phantasies of a "robber woman" who would "take everything out of her." Every detail of her own sadistic phantasies was reflected in the character of her superego.

From the beginning of her work Melanie Klein was impressed by the intensity of the child's anxiety, both conscious and unconscious, and by her need to use violent mechanisms of defense.

The child protects itself against the anxiety produced by threatening internal figures by constantly splitting them off and projecting them outside, and trying to introject idealized parental figures. Abraham assumed that before repression, there may be more violent mechanisms of defense. This is fully borne out in the analysis of children, who use violent ejection and projection in relation both to the internal persecutors and to their own sadism, as well as violent methods of trying to annihilate those projected persecutors and sadistic parts of the self. Thus, by processes of projection and introjection, very active in small children, the child gradually builds up an internal world of ideal and persecutory objects split off from one another, kept far apart. Those phantasies color and distort his perception of his real parents.

Freud discovered the repressed child in the adult. Investigating children, Melanie Klein discovered what was already repressed in the child—namely the infant. As her work progressed, she saw more and more that children were dominated by their unconscious relation to already repressed *part objects* of the oral phase. Freud had assumed that the infant's first relation was to the breast. Abraham observed and described the importance of the relation to part objects such as the breast or feces particularly in his work on melancholia.[4] He followed Freud

[4] K. Abraham, "A Short Study of the Development of the Libido, Viewed in the Light of Mental Disorders" (1924), in *The Selected Papers of Karl Abraham.*

in believing that up to the latter part of the anal phase the child is narcissistic, yet his clinical work brought evidence that the child did relate to early part objects. He suggested that in relation to part objects the child can have "partial love." Melanie Klein attaches even more weight to the part-object relationship. She sees the relation to the breast as of fundamental importance. She describes introjection of a good and a bad breast as the first step in building the infant's inner world. Over the years the term "object" acquired for Klein a meaning somewhat different from that which it had for Freud. Freud sees the object as the object of instincts: Klein sees it more as the object of the infant; an object of instinctual drives certainly, but also an object of dependence, love, hatred—a psychological as well as an instinctual object. Also that object in the infant's mind has psychological features, a personality; and this applies to part objects as well as to people. They can be seen as loving, hating, greedy, envious, and so forth. This perception of the part object as having personal characteristics derives from a combination of the child's experience of his mother's personality and his projections into the object of some of his own feelings. In her later works the differentiation between the relation to and character of part and whole objects became of critical importance. In *The Psycho-Analysis of Children* and in most papers written before 1934, she was still following Abraham's and Freud's views about the phases of libidinal development, and she thought that the child had a first early sucking phase, as described by Abraham, followed by a sadistic, cannibalistic phase. She seemed to accept that in the first phase the breast is all good, and there is no sadism or ambivalence, and that only in the second phase does ambivalence set in, and with it the need to split and project. In other places, however, she states that from the beginning the child, in phantasy, introjects the mother's breast and constantly splits its good and bad aspects, aiming at introjecting a good breast and projecting and annihilating the bad one.

The cannibalistic relation to the breast, which sets in during the second oral stage, is soon transferred to the penis as well. For instance, in Inga, a little girl in the latency period, games used to lead to a representation of an oral relation to both the breast and the penis. "In the further course of the game, however, she preferred to sell me as her customer things to eat for my children, and it became evident that her father's penis and her mother's breast were the objects of her deepest oral desires and that it was her oral frustrations that were at the bottom of her troubles in general and her difficulty in regard to learning in particular."[5] The penis, like the breast, can be split into an ideal one and a very bad one. Erna had phantasies of a very bad penis, but also of one that was "a golden thing." Rita phantasied not only a persecuting *"Butzen,"* but also a very desirable one.

The sadistic, cannibalistic phantasies and anxieties, aggravated by weaning, lead the child to displace its interest on to the whole of its mother's body, and a primitive Oedipal envy and jealousy is added to the oral sadism. Soon urethral and anal sadism are added to the oral, leading to the stage described by Melanie Klein as the stage of maximum sadism.

> Every other vehicle of sadistic attack that the child employs, such as anal sadism and muscular sadism is, in the first instance, levelled against its mother's frustrating breast, but it is soon directed to the inside of her body, which thus becomes at once the target of every highly intensified and effective instrument of sadism. In early analysis these anal-sadistic, destructive desires of the small child constantly alternate with desires to destroy its mother's body by devouring and wetting it,

[5] *Writings* II, p. 62.

but their original aim of eating up and destroying her breast is always discernible in them.[6]

In discovering the child's primitive Oedipus complex she uncovered a whole new world of the child's complex and rich phantasies and anxieties relating to its mother's body. In the child's phantasy the mother's body is full of riches—milk, food, valuable magic feces, babies, and the father's penis, which (in this oral stage of his development) the infant imagines as incorporated by his mother during intercourse. His mother's body stirs in the child powerful desires to explore it and possess himself of its riches. It stirs libidinal desires but also envy and hatred. In phantasy, the infant subjects the mother's body to greedy attacks in which he phantasizes robbing her of these riches, and to envious destructive attacks motivated more by hatred than by desire. Because of these attacks, the mother's body may become the particular object not only of desire and envy but also of hatred and fear. Melanie Klein summarizes thus:

> This envy proved to be the central point of Erna's neurosis. The attacks which she made at the beginning of her analysis as the "third person" on the house which was occupied only by a man and a woman turned out to be a portrayal of her aggressive impulses against her mother's body and her father's penis assumed to be inside it. These impulses, stimulated by the little girl's oral envy, found expression in her game in which she sank the ship (her mother) and tore away from the captain (her father) the "long golden thing" and his head that kept him afloat, i.e. castrated him symbolically as he was copulating with her mother. The details of her phantasies of assault show to what heights of sadistic ingenuity these attacks upon her mother's body went. She would, for instance, transform her excrements into dangerous and explosive substances so as to wreck it from within. This was depicted by the

[6] Ibid, p. 129.

burning down and destruction of the house and the "bursting" of the people inside it. The cutting-out of paper (making "mincemeat" and "eye-salad") represented a complete destruction of the parents in the act of coition. Erna's wish to bite off my nose and to make "fringes" in it was at the same time an attack directed against her father's penis which I was supposed to have incorporated, as was proved by the material produced in other cases. (In other analyses, too, I have found that attacks—whether phantasized or real—upon my nose, feet, head, etc., never referred simply to those parts of my body as such; they were also directed against them as symbolic representations of the father's penis, attached to, or incorporated by me, that is, the mother.)

That Erna, in her phantasy, made attacks on her mother's body with an eye to seizing and destroying the other things also contained therein (i.e. faeces and children) is shown by the variety of fish around which there revolved that desperate struggle, in which every resource was employed, between the "fishwife" (her mother) and me as the child (herself). She furthermore imagined, as we saw, that I, after having to look on while she and the policeman "wurled" money, or fish, together, tried to gain possession of the fish at all costs. The sight of her parents in sexual intercourse had therefore induced a desire to steal her father's penis and whatever else might be inside her mother's body. Erna's reaction against this intention of robbing and completely destroying her mother's body was expressed in the fear she had, after her struggles with the fishwife, that a robber woman would take out everything inside her. It is this fear that I have described as belonging to the earliest danger-situation of the girl and which I consider as an equivalent to the castration anxiety of boys. (See also my "Early Stages of the Oedipus Conflict" [1928, *Writings, 1*] where the connection between the subject's inhibition in work and his sadistic identification with his mother is discussed.)[7]

7 Ibid., p. 56.

This anxiety is a persecutory fear related to the mother's body and the father's penis, as a part object within it, and is seen by Melanie Klein as the dominant anxiety of childhood which it is a central task in the child's development to overcome. The mechanisms for dealing with this anxiety are manifold. There is splitting and idealization of the real parents, as contrasted with the nightmare images, and good idealized parents may be introjected to help against anxiety. There are phantasies of restitution and reparation to the mother's body. There is also a displacing of interest from the mother's body, which stirs so much anxiety, to the world around, and the child begins to develop an interest in the external world.

The anxieties of this phase are of a psychotic nature. Klein agrees with Abraham's opinion that the points of fixation of psychotic illness lie in the oral and early anal phase of development, but she goes further than that. She finds in the child's psychoanalytic material evidence that these fears persist, and considers that the infantile neurosis itself is a defense structure against an anxiety situation which is of a psychotic nature. Thus her theory at this point departs from Freud's. In Freud's view infantile neurosis is initiated by the Oedipus complex and the castration fear, and this may lead, among other defenses, to a regression to pre-genital phases. In Melanie Klein's view the basic anxiety is related to the oral and anal phases and the primitive relation to the mother's body. She sees the infantile neuroses, the phobias, the obsessions, and so on, as defense systems against underlying psychotic anxieties. Thus the bedtime rituals of little Rita, or the complicated obsessions of Erna, were devised to control sadistic impulses and internal persecutors, which gave rise to psychotic paranoid anxieties. (Infantile neurosis should in fact be called "childhood neurosis" as it occurs in children, not infants. Klein describes infantile anxieties underlying the neurotic patterns of the child.)

The way the child deals with his phantasies and anxieties in relation to his mother's body will materially influence the development of his Oedipus complex. The early Oedipal wishes and anxieties relate to the mother's body and the father's penis as a part object.

When the father is perceived more as a separate person, the child's phantasy creates what Klein has termed the combined parental figure. In this phantasy the father is no longer perceived as merely a penis incorporated by the mother, but both parents in intercourse are combined into one figure. This combination serves to deny their intercourse and yet the hatred of such a combination cannot be denied and the child's hatred of the parents' intercourse is projected on to this figure. It becomes a hateful and terrifying figure—the basis of phantasies of many-headed or many-legged monsters which enter into the child's nightmares and fears. The parents in intercourse may be experienced by the child as combined against himself or as attacking one another. Freud noticed that the primal scene (the child's perception or phantasy of the parental intercourse) is always felt by the child as a sadistic one, but he gives no explanation why this should be so. Klein shows that the combined parental figure is imbued with such sadism because of the hatred with which the child experiences it. In her work before 1934, she does not yet clearly use the concept of projective identification, as she will do later on, to account for the hated figure being perceived as a hating one.

Psychoanalytic theory usually develops in the opposite direction to the development of the individual: the study of the adult neurosis led Freud to discover the child in the adult; the study of children led Mrs. Klein to the infant in the child. At the beginning of her work she was struck by the fact that the Oedipus complex made its appearance early, and that pre-genital elements played a large part in it. Analyzing this situation, she came to understand more about the child's primitive relation to the mother's body and to her breast. She could then map the child's development from the earliest relation to the breast to the onset of the Oedipus complex. In 1932, in the last two chapters of *The Psycho-Analysis of Children*, she gives her view of the child's development based on her psychoanalytic experience of adults as well as children.[8] She discusses separately the sexual development of the girl and of the boy. She describes children of both sexes as originally turning from mother's frustrating breast to the father's penis as an object of desire. In the little boy this is the basis of later homosexual trends, but in that he also incorporates and identifies with the desired penis, it also lays a basis for a good heterosexual development. Conversely, in the little girl the oral turning to the father's penis paves the way to genital receptivity, while incorporation and identification with the father's penis contributes to the homosexual trends. Children of both sexes go through the phase of an attack on the mother's body and the incorporated penis and the anxieties of that position influence their further development. In the little girl, if the anxiety about her mother's body and her father's penis inside it is excessive, she may be unable to identify with the mother in a sexual role. The guilt about the attacks on the mother's body stimulates the wish to make restitution to her. This increases the girl's envy of her father's penis, as she perceives the father as able to give to mother pleasure and babies. The penis, in its good aspect, is seen as having

[8] Ibid., pp. 194–278.

reparative functions in relation to the mother's body. If the anxiety is not excessive, the girl may identify with her mother and view her own sexual activity and her wish to have babies not only as a satisfaction of her own desire but also as a restoration of her internal mother.

The little boy also goes through a phase of identification with the desired and envied body of the mother, and of desire for the father's penis, described by Klein as the boy's feminine position. And again, if his mother's body stirs too much anxiety, he may develop hypochondriacal anxieties about his own body in identification with hers. When he identifies with his father and his sexual desires are directed to his mother as an external object, excessive anxiety about the destruction he brought about in her by his omnipotent phantasies may lead to a phobia of the female body. This phobia may extend to symbols of the mother's body, sometimes leading to a general inhibition. For instance, John, aged seven, who suffered from severe intellectual inhibitions, produced the following material:

The next day he showed anxiety and said he had had a bad dream. "The fish was a crab. He was standing on a pier at the seaside where he has often been with his mother. He was supposed to kill an enormous crab which came out of the water on to the pier. He shot it with his little gun and killed it with his sword, which was not very efficient. As soon as he killed the crab, he had to kill more and more of them which kept on coming out of the water." I asked him why he had to do this and he said to stop them going into the world, because they would kill the whole world. As soon as we began on this dream he got into the same position on the table as the day before and kicked harder than ever. I then asked him why he kicked, and he answered, "I am lying on the water and crabs are all around me." The scissors the day before had represented the crabs nipping and cutting him, and this was why he had drawn a boat and a seaplane in which to escape from them. I said he had been on a pier, and he answered,

"Oh yes, but I fell down into the water long ago." The crabs wanted most of all to get into a joint of meat on the water which looked like a house. It was mutton, his favourite meat. He said they had never been inside yet, but they might get in by the doors and windows. The whole scene on the water was the inside of his mother —the world. The meat-house represented both her body and his. The crabs stood for his father's penis and their numbers were legion. They were as big as elephants and were black outside and red inside. They were black because someone had made them black, and so everything had turned black in the water. They had got into the water from the other side of the sea. Someone who had wanted to turn the water black had put them in there. It turned out that the crabs represented not only his father's penis but his own faeces. One of them was no bigger than a lobster and was red outside as well as inside. This represented his own penis. There was much material as well to show that he identified his faeces with dangerous animals which would at his command (by a sort of magic) enter into his mother's body and damage and poison both her and his father's penis.[9]

To John the whole world was his mother's body, and his fear of it extended to the world at large and inhibited his curiosity and capacity to learn. Thus the little boy's castration anxieties spring not only from the Oedipal rivalry with his father but also from the early anxiety about his mother's body and the dangerous penis of his father inside it. If anxiety is not excessive, the little boy can identify with his father's beneficial sexual activity and see genital activity as restoring and refilling his mother's body.

In Freud's view of female sexuality[10] the little girl's development is markedly different from that of the little

[9] *Writings* I, p. 237.
[10] "New Introductory Lectures on Psycho-Analysis," *SE* XXII, pp. 112–35; "An Outline of Psycho-Analysis," *SE* XXIII, p. 193; "Some Psychical Consequences of the Anatomical Distinction between the Sexes," *SE* XIX, pp. 248–58.

boy. He attributes to the girl a long pre-Oedipal fixation to her mother. When genital impulses come into play, the girl, like the boy, takes her mother as the primary object of sexual desire, but she discovers in the phallic phase that she has no penis, and she envies her father and brother theirs. This penis envy, according to Freud, is of crucial importance in the development of the girl and often an important source of pathology. The girl turns away from her mother in great anger. The deep root of the little girl's hatred for mother is her resentment at not having been given a penis.[11] (He notes, however, that whenever women complain of their mothers for not having given them a penis they invariably go on to complain that mother never gave them enough breast feeding, and wonders about the significance of that.) She then turns to her father, having renounced the demand for a penis of her own, and desires a baby from him as an equivalent of the penis. She has also a long period of dormant sexuality, until her discovery of the vagina, which does not happen until puberty. Thus the little boy's Oedipus complex comes to an end because of his castration complex, while in the little girl, on the contrary, the castration complex initiates the Oedipus complex.

Melanie Klein sees both the little boy and the little girl as having a long history of pre-genital attachment to their mothers but does not consider it as necessarily pre-Oedipal. She sees the father entering as an object of desire and rivalry already in the second oral phase. According to her, this oral relation to the father's penis is the precursor of genital feelings, and she attributes to both sexes an early awareness of the vagina and its function. She disagrees with Freud's view of the phallic phase. In her experience, the dominant phantasy of a

11 "Female Sexuality" (1931), *SE* XXI, pp. 225–43.

mother with a penis is part of the phantasies about the mother's body containing the incorporated penis of the father. Klein does not see the little girl as having a long dormant phase of sexuality. She thinks that as soon as the girl turns from her mother's breast to an interest in her mother's body and her father's penis, she enters an active, though to begin with pre-genital, Oedipal conflict. At first she desires and envies her mother's breast; then her possession of her father's penis and babies, and the conflict which this brings with her mother, comes to dominate her phantasies and anxieties.

As the parents become more differentiated and the father becomes desired in his own right, rather than merely as an adjunct of the mother, a more genital form of the Oedipus complex gradually evolves.

By 1932 Klein is already diverging in certain respects from Freud's views on child development. She sees the superego as a much earlier structure, and though she does not explicitly say so, in fact she sees it as a forebear rather than as an heir to the Oedipal complex, since the early introjections of the good and bad breast which enter into the composition of the superego precede the Oedipus complex. She also regards the superego as being more influenced by the child's own instinctual drives than by the real parents. In *Civilization and Its Discontents*, Freud, in one of the very few direct references he makes to Melanie Klein, comments on this view of the nature of the superego: "Experience shows, however, that the severity of the super-ego which a child develops in no way corresponds to the severity of treatment which he has himself met with. The severity of the former seems to be independent of that of the latter (as has rightly been emphasized by Melanie Klein and by other English writers)."[12]

[12] *SE* XXI, p. 130.

From the beginning of her work Klein in various ways linked the severity of the superego to the child's sadistic impulses, either invoking the talion principle (the superego retaliating tooth for tooth) or speaking of the "imprint" of the child's impulses on the superego. In 1933, in her paper "The Early Development of Conscience in the Child,"[13] she states for the first time directly that the child projects his aggressive impulses into his internal object—thus the object becomes punishing, becomes the superego. This concept of projecting into internal objects will acquire increasing importance as her work develops.

Tracing the Oedipus complex back to its pre-genital origin, she sees it as even more complex than Freud had described it. She attributes more importance to the boy's pre-genital development and fixation on his mother, where Freud saw such a fixation as characteristic of little girls only, and she traces the boy's feminine position to his early relation to the mother's body. She views female sexuality differently from Freud—not as a castrated version of male sexuality, but as existing in its own right. She assumes in both sexes an early awareness of the vagina—related also to the phantasies about the mother's body and its functions. She sees as the girl's basic anxiety, her fear that the mother will scoop out her body and destroy its inside, a view also put forward by Jones, who called it "fear of aphanisis."[14] She describes the little girl's penis envy and castration anxiety as part of her whole relation to the mother and father. The little girl first envies the mother her possession of an internalized penis. When the father becomes differentiated, she envies his penis as the instrument which gives

13 *Writings* I, pp. 248–57.
14 E. Jones, "The Early Development of Female Sexuality" (1927) and "The Phallic Phase" (1932), in his *Papers on Psycho-Analysis.*

him power to possess the mother, control her, attack her, or restore her. In the Oedipal situation penis envy is an offshoot of Oedipal jealousy. In the little boy, too, envy of the penis is related to his desire for the mother, and although castration anxiety becomes paramount in the genital phase, earlier fears exist related to the boy's feminine phase—fears of being scooped out and having his inside annihilated. Those early anxieties underlie and add to the castration anxiety proper.

But these differences in view are related to a more fundamental and gradual shift from an emphasis on the vicissitudes of the libido to an emphasis on the complexity of object relationships in phantasy and reality and the interplay between the aggressive and libidinal drives.

It is curious to note that although from very early on in her work Melanie Klein attached cardinal importance to the child's aggressive impulses, she came rather late to the use of Freud's concept of the life and death instincts. This concept was available after 1920, the year in which Freud published "Beyond the Pleasure Principle."[15] In the first part of *The Psycho-Analysis of Children*,[16] based on the lectures given to the British Psychoanalytical Society in 1925, Klein makes no reference to the death instinct, but in the second, theoretical part of the book, written later, she takes as her basis the theory of the life and death instincts and describes the child's development in terms of conflict between libidinal and destructive forces. There is no mention of the death instinct in her first paper on the Oedipus complex written in 1928, but it plays a large part in the chapter, "Early Stages of the Oedipus Conflict and of Super-Ego Formation" in *The Psycho-Analysis of Children*. In her papers the first clear

[15] *SE* XVIII
[16] *Writings* II

reference to the death instinct comes in 1933, in "The Early Development of Conscience in the Child."[17] It is there too that she first distinguishes more clearly between anxiety and guilt. She says that anxiety pertains to the persecutory fear of the superego into which the child's aggression was projected, whereas guilt arises later when the severity of the superego has been mitigated and concern for the object becomes stronger than anxiety.

In the main, Klein's views on the child's Oedipus complex—specifically her assertion that it starts in the second half of the oral stage—were confirmed by her later work and remained generally unaltered. Nor did she vary from her early insights about the importance of the attacks on the mother's body and phantasies about the mother's body and the parental couple. Her discoveries about the girl's feminine development and the boy's feminine phase were also confirmed in her later work. Some of her thinking, however, underwent change after her discovery of the central importance of the depressive position. Up until 1934 she thought that the Oedipus complex began at the phase of maximum sadism and was stimulated by the trauma of weaning, and therefore started under the prevalence of hatred. This view she subsequently altered. She abandoned the view of the phase of maximum sadism and though she still placed the beginnings of the Oedipus complex in the second oral stage, she now connected it with the depressive position and therefore with a conflict betwen love and hatred in which love played a very important role.

17 *Writings* I, pp. 248–57.

V

The period 1919 to 1934 may be considered as the first phase of Melanie Klein's development. What is its importance in relation to the whole of her work? She had in those years discovered and described the complexities of the early pre-genital Oedipus complex and the origins and evolution of the superego, tracing it also to pre-genital roots. She had discovered the importance of splitting, projection, and introjection, and had described with great detail and accuracy the gradual building up of the child's internal world. She had understood the importance of the oral phase and its lasting influence on later development, and also the importance of the psychotic anxieties which underlie the childhood neuroses.

Klein's views about anxiety, to which she always paid a great deal of attention, evolved as her work progressed. In her early papers she followed Freud in assuming that the child's principal anxiety always concerns castration, but increasingly she came to view it as a fear of a persecutory attack by parents who have themselves been attacked by the child in phantasy, particularly in relation to the primal scene; castration anxiety is one manifestation of this more general fear. She relates anxiety to fear of retaliation. In 1933 in her paper "The Early Development of Conscience in the Child"[1] she states clearly that persecutory anxiety is due to the child's projections of his own destructive impulses. At that time Freud, in the course of reformulating his ideas about anxiety, also attributed a much greater role to the operation of aggression and the death instinct than he had done in his earlier work.[2]

As her work progressed, certain other fundamental concepts of Freud on which it was based, such as that of unconscious phantasy and symbolism, became gradually enlarged and altered. Freud seems to consider unconscious phantasy as a relatively late mental product, coming when the reality principle is established and the pleasure principle goes on operating in a split-off way. "With the introduction of the reality principle one species of thought-activity was split off; it was kept free from reality-testing and remained subordinated to the pleasure principle alone. This activity is *phantasying*."[3] Klein, in her work with little children, observed that unconscious phantasy was early, ubiquitous, and dynamic, influencing all the child's perceptions and object relationships. This view of phantasy as having fundamental importance was also linked with a change of emphasis from the theory of phases of libidinal development to that of

[1] *Writings* I, pp. 248–57.
[2] "Inhibitions, Symptoms and Anxiety," *SE* XX, pp. 87–174.
[3] "Formulations Regarding the Two Principles of Mental Functioning," *SE* XII, p. 222.

the development of object relations. She had observed in small children that object relations, both with reality objects and particularly with phantasy objects, are operative from as far back as one can discern, and, furthermore, that the early part-object relation to the mother's breast/body and to the father's penis played a very important part in the structure of the child's internal objects, its superego, and its phantasy life.

The concept of internal objects acquired an increasing importance in her work. Freud had described an internal object in the mental structure, the superego, as an introjected parental figure. Klein expanded this concept. She discovered that in phantasy the infant introjects such objects as the mother's breast, the father's penis, and other parts of the parental bodies. In time, the combined parental figure, later on the parents together in intercourse but not combined into one, and eventually the parents as separate people, are internalized. These internal objects are not exact replicas of real external objects, but are always colored by the infant's phantasy and projections. They can become split into ideal and persecutory objects, such as good breasts and bad ones. Also they can become more integrated. There are introjects of part objects and of parents as whole people, sometimes very distorted in phantasy, but gradually becoming more realistic as the child's relation to reality improves. These internal objects are experienced as having relations both to one another and to the child itself. The child may identify with such objects, or feel itself as being in a relationship with them. In her earlier work Klein called "superego" all internal objects which the child was not identified with. Later, seeing the complexity of the relationship to the internal objects, she speaks more often of internal objects, their character and functions, reserving the term "superego" only for the punitive aspect of objects. In her work before 1934 it is not quite clear how the earlier introjects relate to the later ones. It is only with the formulation of the depressive position (a concept I shall explain in chapter vii) that Klein came to describe in a more systematic way the evolution and integration of the internal objects.

Her emphasis on the relationships to objects, external and internal, was such that her views became known as an "object relation theory." Now, when it is more usual to speak of "Kleinian" theory or viewpoint, the term "object relation theory" refers more often to the theories of Donald Winnicott, Michael Balint, and particularly W. R. D. Fairbairn, who, in contrast to Melanie Klein, departed completely from Freud's instinct theory.

The change of emphasis in relation to the functioning of unconscious phantasy went with certain changes in the concept of symbolism. The unconcious phantasy of the child, she observed, expresses itself in a symbolical way in its play and all its activities. In an early paper entitled "The Role of the School in the Libidinal Development of the Child" (1923)[4] she describes how unconscious phantasies underlie the child's schoolwork and how all the school activities as well as free play contain a symbolic expression of the child's phantasy life. In that paper she describes how, for many children, the school building itself may represent the mother's body with the teacher, representing the father, inside it. Then all activities at school may be felt as penetrations into the mother's body. The work itself, she shows, has symbolical meaning—for instance, individual numbers or letters may represent sexual organs. In two patients, for example, the "i" stood for the penis and the "e" for the vagina. For another, the "l" and the "o" represented masculine and feminine organs. Putting these letters or num-

4 *Writings* I, pp. 59–76.

bers together represented intercourse. In the first part of her paper she relates inhibitions in school activities mainly to castration anxiety; she goes on to introduce other elements, both aggressive and pre-genital.

> Fritz had a marked inhibition in doing division sums, all explanations proving unavailing, for he understood them quite well but always did these sums wrong. He told me once that in doing division he had first of all to bring down the figure that was required and he climbed up, seized it by the arm and pulled it down. To my enquiry as to what it said to that, he replied that quite certainly it was not pleasant for the number —it was as if his mother stood on a stone 13 yards high and someone came and caught her by the arm so that they tore it out and divided her. Shortly before-hand, however, he had phantasied about a woman in the circus who was sawn in pieces and then neverthe-less comes to life again, and now he asked me whether this is possible. He then related (also in connection with a previously elaborated phantasy) that actually every child wants to have a bit of his mother, who is to be cut into four pieces; he depicted quite exactly how she screamed and had paper stuffed in her mouth so she could not scream and what kind of faces she made, etc. A child took a very sharp knife and he de-scribed how she was cut up; first across the width of the breast and then up the belly and then lengthwise so that the "pipi" (penis), the faeces and the head were cut exactly through the middle, whereby the "sense" (the "sense" was the penis) was taken out of her head.[5]

After the interpretation of those phantasies his inhibi-tions in regard to division completely disappeared. An-other child, Greta, saw parsing in grammar as an actual dismembering and dissection of a roast rabbit—which often represented her mother's breast and genital.

From the beginning of her work, Klein saw the child as

[5] Ibid., pp. 69–70.

actively symbolizing, in his activities in the external world, his phantasies about his parents and siblings; and she regarded symbolism as the basis of all sublimation. Her view of symbolism was enriched and made more explicit when she began to study in detail the child's relation to the mother's body and the anxieties stirred by his phantasied attacks. In 1930 she published the crucial paper "The Importance of Symbol-Formation in the Development of the Ego." There she states:

Ferenczi holds that identification, the forerunner of symbolism, arises out of the baby's endeavour to rediscover in every object his own organs and their functioning. In Jones's view the pleasure-principle makes it possible for two quite different things to be equated because of a similarity marked by pleasure or interest. Some years ago I wrote a paper, based on these concepts, in which I drew the conclusion that symbolism is the foundation of all sublimation and of every talent, since it is by way of symbolic equation that things, activities and interests become the subject of libidinal phantasies.

I can now add to what I said then (1923b) and state that, side by side with the libidinal interest, it is the anxiety arising in the phase that I have described which sets going the mechanism of identification. Since the child desires to destroy the organs (penis, vagina, breasts) which stand for the objects, he conceives a dread of the latter. This anxiety contributes to make him equate the organs in question with other things; owing to this equation these in their turn become objects of anxiety, and so he is impelled constantly to make other and new equations, which form the basis of his interest in the new objects and of symbolism.

Thus, not only does symbolism come to be the foundation of all phantasy and sublimation but, more than that, it is the basis of the subject's relation to the outside world and to reality in general. I pointed out that the object of sadism at its height, and of the desire for knowledge arising simultaneously with sadism, is the mother's body with its phantasied contents.[6]

She paid a great deal of attention both in her clinical work and her theoretical formulations to the child's developing interest in the external world and his desire for knowledge. She considered the impulse to search for knowledge (epistemophilia) so fundamental that up to 1934 she used the term "epistemophilic instinct." Later on she dropped that term as she came more and more to see all behavior in terms of the basic life and death instincts, and the epistemophilic drive derives from both. Freud treated curiosity about the world as a derivative of the component scoptophilic instinct (voyeurism), and up to a point, Klein's view is in keeping with Freud's in that she considers an interest in the world to be a displacement from the basic interest in one's own and the parents' bodies; but she attaches to it a far greater importance. The wish to explore as well as to possess or attack the mother's body is for her the mainspring of the whole epistemophilic relation to the world, symbolism being the link between the two. External objects are in the first place symbols of the child's and the parents' bodies or parts of them.

The paper is based on the analysis of a psychotic boy, Dick. Dick at the age of four had no symbolic activities. He did not talk and did not play. He had also no affective relationship with his objects. He did not react to the presence or absence of his parents or nanny and showed no anxiety. He did however show a rudimentary interest in door handles, in the opening and closing of doors, and in railway stations. Utilizing this interest, Klein was able to get in contact with him and start an analysis. As it progressed, he began to experience anxiety, for instance,

[6] Ibid., pp. 220–21.

whenever his nanny left him in the consulting room, and he also began to develop a relationship to the people around him. He then started speaking. Dick showed in his play that in his phantasy he made sadistic attacks on his mother's body which filled him with overpowering anxiety. For instance, he got Mrs. Klein to cut pieces of wood out of a toy cart, whereupon he immediately became anxious and threw away the damaged cart and its contents, saying, "Gone." He then hid in an empty cupboard. Later, when he came upon the damaged cart and the bits of wood representing coal in the cart, he quickly threw both aside and covered them with other toys.

> As his analysis progressed it became clear that in thus throwing them out of the room he was indicating an expulsion, both of the damaged object and of his own sadism (or the means employed by it), which was in this manner projected into the external world. Dick had also discovered the wash-basin as symbolizing the mother's body, and he displayed an extraordinary dread of being wetted with water. He anxiously wiped it off his hand and mine, which he had dipped in as well as his own, and immediately afterwards he showed the same anxiety when urinating. Urine and faeces represented to him injurious and dangerous substances.[7]

The enormous anxiety that Dick experienced made him withdraw all interest from his mother's body and any object that would symbolize it. Thus, both his phantasy life and his interest in external reality came to a stop.

> Dick cut himself off from reality and brought his phantasy-life to a standstill by taking refuge in the phantasies of the dark, empty mother's body. He had thus succeeded in withdrawing his attention also from the different objects in the outside world which represented the contents of the mother's body—the father's penis, faeces, children. His own penis, as the organ of

[7] Ibid., p. 226.

sadism, and his own excreta were to be got rid of (or denied) as being dangerous and aggressive.[8]

When Mrs. Klein got in touch with those phantasies and the child's unconscious anxiety diminished and became more conscious, the symbolic process was set in motion. As the analysis expanded and Dick's playing became richer, it became clear to Mrs. Klein that excessive guilt, which at that time she related to premature genitality, as well as anxiety was a critical inhibiting factor. (In this she followed Abraham, in whose view the concern for the object belongs to the genital phase.)

The importance of this paper is manifold. It opened the way to the analysis of psychotics—until then inaccessible to analysis because of their inability to communicate in symbolic terms. It also gave a new stimulus to the study of the pathology of childhood. At that time psychosis in children was very seldom diagnosed and often went unrecognized. Klein drew attention to the fact that it was much more frequent than was acknowledged, and showed that it could be treatable. (Dick was diagnosed as a schizophrenic. It was years later that Kanner[9] described the syndrome as early infantile autism, which is probably how Dick would be diagnosed today.) Klein's interest in childhood psychoses was a natural extension of her work. She had repeatedly found that psychotic features are often pronounced in the infantile neurosis. Another important contribution in this paper relates to anxiety; here Klein gives the clearest statement that anxiety, if not excessive, is an essential spur to the child's development.

But above all, this paper was seminal for the study of symbolism, both creative and pathological; it gave a new

[8] Ibid., p. 227.
[9] L. Kanner, "Autistic Disturbances of Affective Contact," *The Nervous Child* 2 (1943), pp. 217–50.

impetus to the investigation of symbol formation, its inhibitions and its misfunctions. In making explicit her views on symbolism, Klein compares and contrasts them to those of Ernest Jones. Jones, in his paper "The Theory of Symbolism,"[10] differentiates between the common speech meaning of "symbol," say a flag symbolizing a country, and the technical, psychoanalytic use of the term to denote "true unconscious symbolism." In that usage a symbol represents what has been repressed from consciousness, and the whole process of symbolization is carried out unconsciously. "Only what is repressed is symbolized; only what is repressed needs to be symbolized."[11] Symbolism is a result of intrapsychic conflict. *"All symbols represent ideas of the self and the immediate blood relatives, or of the phenomena of birth, love and death."*[12] (Jones's italics.) Although many, and different, symbols can be used to represent the same repressed idea, any given symbol has a constant and universal meaning. Jones further distinguishes between sublimation and symbolization: symbols arise when the "affect investing the symbolised idea has not, in so far as the symbolism is concerned, proved capable of that modification in quality denoted by the term 'sublimation'."[13] Melanie Klein certainly agrees with Freud's and Jones's fundamental tenets that it is primary objects and functions that are objects of symbolization, and that symbolization is due to an intrapsychic conflict linked with repression. She contributes to the understanding of this process, describing in detail and with clinical material how symbols are formed as a result of the conflict, and delineating the role played in this process by anxiety and

[10] E. Jones, *Papers on Psycho-Analysis*, pp. 87–144.
[11] Ibid., p. 116.
[12] Ibid., p. 102.
[13] Ibid., p. 139.

guilt. A feature of particular interest in her paper is that she shows symbolism in *statu nascendi*. But the difference between her view and Jones's is perhaps greater than she was aware of at the time. Jones viewed symbols as immutable, Klein sees them as overdetermined, one symbol often containing many meanings. She also views symbolization not as an alternative to sublimation but as a basis and essential part of all sublimation. At first sight it may seem that by extending the idea of unconscious symbolism to include sublimation she loses Freud's and Jones's distinction between the common speech usage of the term and the psychoanalytic usage. This, however, is not the case. She does speak of "true unconscious symbolism" as defined by Jones—the outcome of repression and intrapsychic conflict in which the referent is always unconscious—but shows that this unconscious symbolism is an essential link between primitive phantasy and the relation to reality.

In one respect her formulation does fall short of clarity. Quoting Ferenczi, who considers that all symbolism arises out of a projection of the child's own body into the external objects, she describes how Dick projects parts of himself into his mother and equates them with parts of her body. Yet Klein also says that it is the mother's body that is explored and symbolized, and she lays a great deal of stress on introjection. That interaction could only be clarified later with her description of projective identification, and her distinction between the paranoid-schizoid and the depressive mode of functioning. These theoretical developments also brought more precision to the understanding of the processes whereby symbolization can give rise either to pathology or sublimation.

The change of emphasis from the phases of libidinal development to anxiety; the new stress on object relations and the child's internal world; the altered view of phantasy and symbolism—all these factors suggest that the first phase of her work was nearing its end, and that she was ready for some more fundamental formulation of her theory. The moment came in 1935 with her paper "A Contribution to the Psychogenesis of Manic-Depressive States."[14]

[14] *Writings* I, pp. 262–89.

The British Psychoanalytical Society

VI

The years 1926 to 1936 were very productive and relatively peaceful for Melanie Klein. One great tragedy which marked them was the sudden death in a mountaineering accident of her eldest son, Hans, in 1933. The mourning for this son, reawakening also her mourning for her lost siblings, Sidonie and Emmanuel, probably contributed to her increasing interest in mourning and depression. In her paper of 1940[1] she uses some of her own dreams to illustrate the processes of mourning. Another sorrow of that period was the bad relationship which developed between her and her daughter, Dr. Melitta Schmideberg, who qualified as an analyst in Berlin and came to London in 1932 with her husband, Dr. Walter Schmideberg.

But despite these problems and sorrows, Melanie

[1] "Mourning and Its Relation to Manic-Depressive States," *Writings* I, pp. 344–69.

Klein was happy in the British Psychoanalytical Society. In those years it was an ideal setting for her
work and gave her support, cooperation, and stimulation of a kind which she had completely lacked in Berlin
since the death of Abraham. When Klein joined the British Society a great deal of original work was already in
progress. There was much interest in the early stages of
development. Jones's early studies on superstition gave
him an insight into the most primitive modes of mental
functioning. He also contributed greatly to the study of
the anal character. Even before Klein's arrival, certain
differences had appeared between the trends of development in Vienna and in London. For instance, Jones was
doubtful about the existence of the phallic phase, and,
like Klein, considered the phallic phase structure to be
defensive. He disagreed with Freud's opinion that castration fear was central and unique, the fear of which all
others are derivative. On the contrary, he was so firmly
convinced of the existence of a basic anxiety that at one
point he even thought of calling it an instinct of fear. He
considered that there was a fundamental anxiety about
losing all sources of libidinal gratification, which he called
"fear of aphanisis," and that castration was the genital
aspect of this basic fear. He thought also that his Viennese colleagues attached too little importance to aggression as compared with libido.

There was in the British Society a lively interest in
work with children. Nina Searle had already started working with children and Sylvia Payne read a paper on child
analysis, although she herself had never analyzed a child.
Susan Isaacs came to analysis from the field of education
and Donald Winnicott from pediatrics. So that when, in
1924, Alix Strachey, who was then in Berlin, sent a report
to the British Society on Melanie Klein's work with children, it excited a lot of interest. As a result of this report

Klein was invited in 1925 to London to give a series of six lectures on child analysis.

When Melanie Klein eventually settled in London she quickly found friends, collaborators, pupils, and analysands, among them many eminent psychoanalysts. Quite a few, including Donald Winnicott, learned her child technique. Joan Riviere and Susan Isaacs became her close friends and collaborators, to be joined later by Paula Heimann.

So Melanie Klein's work was in harmony with the trends of development in the British Society and the influence of her discoveries was far-reaching. This is reflected in *The International Journal of Psycho-Analysis* in which many papers (some of them on analysis of children) bear witness to her influence. After the publication of *The Psycho-Analysis of Children* (1932)[2] Edward Glover wrote a ten-page review in the *International Journal of Psycho-Analysis*,[3] from which it is apparent that he considered this book a milestone in the development of psychoanalysis. He says:

> And I have no hesitation in stating that in two main respects her book is of fundamental importance for the future of psycho-analysis. It contains not only unique clinical material gathered from first-hand analytic observations of children, but lays down certain conclusions which are bound to influence both the theory and practice of analysis for some time to come.

Glover makes certain criticisms—mostly well-founded. Making a book out of two series of lectures led to overlapping and repetition. *The Psycho-Analysis of Children* is admittedly not very well written. On matters of substance, he commends Mrs. Klein for drawing attention to the importance of aggression, but sounds a note of

[2] *Writings* II.
[3] *Int. J. Psycho-Anal.* 14 (1933), pp. 119–29.

warning about possible underestimation of the libidinal forces. This, indeed, is a bias which remained with Mrs. Klein until her formulation of the depressive position, when she redresses this imbalance. He also says that she errs in following too closely Abraham's schema of libidinal phases of development, and in particular in admitting the first oral preambivalent stage, for which there is no clinical evidence. That too was a view Mrs. Klein was to abandon when she came to formulate her theory of the paranoid-schizoid position.

On the whole, Melanie Klein's development and that of the British Society went hand in hand. Divergences between London and Vienna were increasing and were now giving Ernest Jones some concern, and to discuss them he organized a series of exchange lectures with the Vienna Society. The first of these was Jones's paper on "Early Female Sexuality,[4] presented in Vienna in 1935, in which he describes as the little girl's deepest anxiety the fear of an attack on the inside of her body by a bad mother, leading to complete aphanisis—the phallic position being a defense against this anxiety. He relates his work to Melanie Klein's and makes use of her findings. The second paper in this series was read by Joan Riviere on "The Genesis of Psychical Conflict in Earliest Infancy," in 1936[5] and was in response to a paper read by R. Wälder to the British Society in the same year.[6] Riviere's paper followed Melanie Klein's paper on the manic-depressive states[7] and offered a most moving description of the depressive position.

[4] *Papers on Psycho-Analysis,* pp. 485–95.
[5] *Int. J. Psycho-Anal. 17* (1936), pp. 395–422.
[6] "The Problem of Freedom in Psycho-Analysis and the Problem of Reality Testing," ibid, pp. 89–108. He replied to J. Riviere's paper in "The Problem of the Genesis of Psychical Conflict in Earliest Infancy," *Int. J. Psycho-Anal. 18* (1937), pp. 406–73.
[7] "A Contribution to the Psychogenesis of Manic-Depressive States," *Writings* I, pp. 262–89.

Up to the time when Mrs. Klein read in the Society her paper on the psychogenesis of the manic-depressive states, one could not speak of a distinctive Kleinian school. There was rather an English school of psychoanalysis, diverging somewhat from the Viennese and Berlin schools, and within the school members could be more or less in agreement with certain or all of Melanie Klein's findings. This, however, began to change in 1935 when she introduced the concept of the depressive position.

The Depressive Position

vii

"A Contribution to the Psychogenesis of Manic-Depressive States"[1] is a watershed in the development of Melanie Klein's thought. In this paper she introduces the entirely new concept of the depressive position. Her work with children had convinced her of the importance of the first years of life for the further development of the child's psychic apparatus and this was confirmed by her work with adults. This understanding was linked with her appreciation of the importance of the internal objects and of the way the child structures the objects he internalizes in the first years of his life. But she had no clear theoretical framework in which to encompass her findings. In "A Contribution to the Psychogenesis of Manic-Depressive States," she examines the primitive

[1] *Writings* I, pp. 262–89.

object relationships and delineates the development from the most primitive part-object relationships to the relationship to whole, separate, external objects. She also differentiates between paranoid and depressive anxieties. As she had often shown in her work with small children, the infant's first relationship is to part objects— primarily the mother's breast. These part objects are split into an ideal breast—the object of the child's desire— and the persecutory breast, an object of hatred and fear, usually seen as fragmented.

In her 1935 paper she states that in the second quarter of the first year, with his growing integration, the child begins to perceive his mother as a whole person. She describes this change as the beginning of the depressive position. She explains that she uses the term "position" rather than "phase" or "stage" because this change signifies that the child begins to experience his object relationship from a different position, a different point of view. When the mother can be seen as a whole object, the infant can love her as a whole person and identify with her in a different way. It is to this whole, loved mother that the child turns to relieve his persecutory fears; he wants to introject her so that she may protect him from inner and outer persecution. This whole, loved mother is, however, herself felt to be an object exposed to constant danger. If she is felt as protecting the infant from the persecutors, by the same token she is exposed to their attack. But that is not all. The mother is now felt to be a whole object not only in contrast to the part objects of the previous state but also in the sense of not being split into a persecutory and an ideal object; she is felt to be the source both of the infant's gratifications and of his frustrations and pain.

His love for her is therefore very ambivalent and easily turns to hatred, so the loved and needed mother is always in danger of being destroyed, not only by the phantasied persecutors but also by the infant's own hatred and sadism. In that she is constantly introjected, the destruction is at the same time an internal one, and the infant's inner world is in ruin and chaos. In that the mother is loved and identified with, the loss of her is felt acutely and a new set of feelings makes its appearance. "Through this step the ego arrives at a new position, which forms the foundation of the situation called the loss of the loved object. Not until the object is loved *as a whole,* can this loss be felt as a whole."[2] (Klein's italics.)

To the feeling of loss and sorrow and pining is added the feeling of guilt: the infant experiences the psychic reality of the danger to the internal object as being due to his own impulses and phantasies. The depressive position is a mixture of paranoid anxieties deriving from the operation of phantasied persecutors of the earlier phase, and depressive feelings of guilt, loss, and pining. In this phase of development the ego feels insecure in the possession of good internal objects. Children and adults suffering from depression in which they regress to the depressive position have a dread of containing dying and dead objects. This is the core of their distress and anxiety.

There is a constant fluctuation between the persecutory anxiety, when hatred is stronger, and the depressive anxiety, when love comes more to the fore. In this connection Klein describes such common symptoms as children's eating difficulties and hypochondriacal anxieties in both children and adults. In children, the feeding difficulties may be linked with paranoid fears of incorporating bad food or with depressive fears of endangering their good object by cannibalistically eating it. She gives clinical material from a hypochondriacal patient, showing the change in his feeling about his symptoms. To begin

[2] Ibid., p. 264.

with, his fears were for himself; he feared being poisoned or destroyed. As, in his analysis, the depressive position became more evident, his hypochondriacal fears were experienced in a different way. He spoke of his poor, endangered organs and the need to nurse them in a way which made it clear that these organs represented the injured objects he had to care for.

The fixation point of paranoia she places before the depressive position—the depressive position in its early phases being the fixation point of melancholia. The melancholic, according to Klein, is in the throes of the depressive position, finding himself unable to establish securely a good internal object. The severity of his super-ego she links with the persecution of the still active paranoid fears plus the reproaches of the good introjected dying or dead objects and their demands to be restituted to an ideal state. The central task of the infant's elaboration of the depressive position is to establish in the core of his ego a sufficiently good and secure whole internal object. If this fails, the child is exposed to mental illness of the paranoid or manic-depressive kind. Hence, the depressive position marks the crossroads of development between the point of fixation of psychoses and that of neuroses.

In the course of the depressive position, new defenses are developed. Before its onset the main defenses against persecutors are splitting of the good and bad objects, idealization, violent expulsion, and annihilation of persecutors and of hateful parts of the self. The depressive position mobilizes additional defenses of a manic nature. In essence, those defenses are directed against experiencing the psychic reality of the depressive pain, and their main characteristic is a denial of psychic reality. Dependence on the object and ambivalence are denied and the object is omnipotently controlled and treated with triumph and contempt so that the loss of the object shall not give rise to pain or guilt. Alternately, or simultaneously, there may be a flight to the idealized internal object, denying any feeling of destruction and loss. Those defenses are part of normal development, but if they are excessive and long-lasting, they impede the growth of a relationship to a good and whole object and the working through of the depressive position.

In *The Psycho-Analysis of Children*, Klein had described a number of restitutive or reparative mechanisms, but it is only with her concept of the depressive position that she came to see reparation as playing a fundamental role in development. The depressive pain, with the guilt and pining for the recovery of the good object, externally and internally, mobilizes reparative wishes and phantasies of restoring the good internal object. It is on those wishes that the establishment of a good internal object hinges. Klein expands that aspect of her work on the depressive position in the companion paper, "Mourning and Its Relation to Manic-Depressive States" (1940),[3] in which she describes how the child builds up his internal world, how his good objects are felt to be destroyed, externally and internally, when his own hatred and sadism are active, and how he tries to rebuild them by his love. The reappearance of his mother and her care for him are essential to this process. Her reappearance reassures him about the strength and resilience of his objects and over and above that, it lessens his belief in the omnipotence of his hostility and increases his trust in his own love and reparative powers. The nonappearance of his mother or the lack of her love can leave him at the mercy of his depressive and persecutory fears.

In studying the processes of normal and abnormal mourning in the adult, Klein came to the conclusion that the disappearance of a loved object in adult life—an

[3] Ibid., pp. 344–69.

object which at a deeper level represents always a parental or sibling figure—reawakens in the mourner the conflicts of the depressive position. Because of the loss of the good external object and the reassurance its presence gave him, and with the increase of hatred toward that object for having left him, the mourner finds himself confronted not only with the pain of having lost the real external object but also, like the infant in the depressive position, under threat of losing the good objects in his internal world. He is exposed to his primitive paranoid and depressive fears. Observation makes us familiar with these kinds of reactions in mourners who seek to blame in a paranoid way doctors or nurses, say, for the death of the loved one, or who experience self-reproaches and self-devaluation in a truly melancholic way. Manic defenses are also mobilized by mourning. As a defense against the pain of loss, unconscious contempt and triumph can be mobilized. This, in turn, increases the guilt, making it harder to restore in one's mind the lost person as a good internal object, and it adds to the pain and length of the work of mourning.

In Freud's view, the work of mourning consists in reality-testing—in the mourner discovering and rediscovering over and over again that the loved person does not exist in the external world—and he says that it is difficult to understand why this process is so painful. Melanie Klein takes it further. She sees this reality-testing not only in relation to rediscovering the absence in the external world but also in relation to one's internal world and the state of one's original internal objects with whom the lost loved person was identified. This work involves the overcoming of regressions to paranoid feelings and to manic defenses until the inner world is restored. If the bereaved person has not been able to overcome the anxieties of his depressive position in the course of his development, he may be incapable of the work of mourning, and abnormal mourning and mental illness may result. If he has been able to do so, the mourning experience can lead to enrichment.

> To conclude. In normal mourning, as well as in abnormal mourning and in manic-depressive states, the infantile depressive position is reactivated. The complex feelings, phantasies and anxieties included under this term are of a nature which justifies my contention that the child in his early development goes through a transitory manic-depressive stage as well as a state of mourning, which become modified by the infantile neurosis. With the passing of the infantile neurosis, the infantile depressive position is overcome.
>
> The fundamental difference between normal mourning, on the one hand, and abnormal mourning and manic-depressive states on the other, is this: the manic-depressive and the person who fails in the work of mourning, though their defences may differ widely from each other, have this in common, that they have been unable in early childhood to establish their internal "good" objects and to feel secure in their inner world. They have never really overcome the infantile depressive position. In normal mourning, however, the early depressive position, which had become revived through the loss of the loved object, becomes modified again, and is overcome by methods similar to those used by the ego in childhood. The individual is reinstating his actually lost loved object; but he is also at the same time re-establishing inside himself his first loved objects—ultimately the "good" parents—whom, when the actual loss occurred, he felt in danger of losing as well. It is by reinstating inside himself the "good" parents as well as the recently lost person, and by rebuilding his inner world, which was disintegrated and in danger, that he overcomes his grief, regains security, and achieves true harmony and peace.[4]

In the 1940 paper Melanie Klein emphasizes the creative aspects of the depressive position; she describes how, at the height of his depressive anxieties, the infant

[4] Ibid., p. 369.

mobilizes his love and his capacities and skill to re-create the good internal state and, as the omnipotence gradually diminishes, also endeavors to make reparation to external objects. She sees in the overcoming of the depressive position a great enrichment of the ego in good internal objects and a major source of sublimation and creative endeavor. In successful mourning in adult life, a similar enrichment can occur.

Mourning which reawakens the distress and anxiety of the depressive position revives also the early Oedipal conflict. Patient D, whose clinical material Klein reports in "Mourning and Its Relation to Manic-Depressive States," had the following dream on the night before his mother's death (which he was expecting):

> *He saw a bull lying in a farmyard. It was not quite dead, and looked very uncanny and dangerous. He was standing on one side of the bull, his mother on the other. He escaped into a house, feeling that he was leaving his mother behind in danger and that he should not do so; but he vaguely hoped that she would get away.*[5] [Klein's italics.]

The associations to this dream indicate that he saw his mother's death as the result of a violent bad intercourse with the bull/father—the father himself being in danger (the bull in the dream is nearly dead). As was shown by his association of a man threatened by the bull, the patient felt himself to be in danger as well; this was due to the internalization of his parents' dangerous intercourse, in which they were destroying one another. After his mother's death, the patient dreamed of a bus driving itself in an uncontrolled way, and entering a shed, which "was going to blazes."[6] The bus, as his associations showed, represented himself.

The dying or dead mother in his internal world was

---

[5] Ibid., p. 364.
[6] Ibid., p. 366.

experienced as having been destroyed either by his own violent sexual impulses or by his father, into whom he projected his violence. (We shall return to this material and discuss it in greater detail in chapter x.)

In her paper "The Oedipus Complex in the Light of Early Anxieties"[7] (1945), Klein describes the interrelationship between the depressive position and the Oedipus complex. She holds to her earlier view that the relation to the breast materially influences the Oedipus complex and that both the little boy and the little girl turn to the father's penis as an alternative object. Nor does she alter her view on the importance of the attack the child makes in phantasy on the mother's body and the parental couple, as shown for example by D. But whereas she thought originally that the Oedipus complex starts in a state in which hatred predominates, the clarification of the depressive position causes her to alter this view. She now sees the beginning of the Oedipus complex as being part and parcel of the depressive position. When the mother is experienced as a whole object, her relation to the father comes into the picture and the Oedipus complex begins in the setting of the depressive position. The whole relation to the breast will influence the relation to the parental couple, but conversely, the Oedipal jealousy, added to the original ambivalence to the breast, will further endanger the relation to the good internal breast. In the depressive position both parents, separately and as a couple, are the child's good whole objects and both are attacked in phantasy, particularly when they are coupled in intercourse.

In earlier papers Klein had described the fears to which those attacks give rise, but with the discovery of the importance of the depressive position, she puts more weight on love and feelings of guilt and loss. Whereas Freud

[7] Ibid., pp. 370–419.

says that the Oedipal wishes are given up through the threat of castration, she states that it is not only anxieties—fear of castration or aphanisis and even death— that makes the child give up his Oedipal wishes but also his love for the parents and his wish not to damage them. The reparative wishes stirred by his depressive anxieties make him long to restore the parents, to overcome his wish to make their intercourse into a destructive act, and to restore it to an act of love and mutual creativity. The child's sexual wishes then become carriers of reparative phantasies. In the Oedipal situation, the boy wishes to identify with the potent father in order to restore the mother and give her babies in sexual intercourse. For instance, in the material of Richard, a ten-year-old child, one can see repeatedly how he made such an attempt and then failed in it, because in his phantasy his father's penis was so often destructive and babies such monsters. It was only toward the end of his treatment that he could begin to identify with a beneficent, reparative father.[8] The little girl, in her desire for a good intercourse, seeks not only her own satisfaction, but also the restoration of her internal mother.

Klein's work on the depressive position is both a continuation of Freud's and Abraham's researches in that area and the culmination of her own work with children and adults. Freud, in his paper on "Mourning and Melancholia" (1917),[9] made the discovery that the melancholic's self-reproaches are mutual reproaches between the ego and the ambivalently introjected internal object. (It was the study of melancholia that first led him to the formulation of the concept of the superego.) He differentiates between melancholia and normal mourning. Melancholia refers to a relation to an internal object, whereas

[8] Idem, and "Narrative of a Child Analysis," *Writings* IV.
[9] *SE* XIV, pp. 237–60.

mourning refers to the loss of an external object. He sees the psychic work of mourning as a repeated rediscovery in the external world that the loved object is no longer there. In mourning, the libido gets gradually detached from the lost object and is free for investment in a new object. The state of the ego itself is not affected by this process. By contrast, in melancholia the object is introjected and the libido is turned inward. But the relation to this internal object is very ambivalent, and a relationship of mutual torture and reproaches is set up within the ego; this results in self-devaluation, hypochondriacal states, and self-reproaches. Though Freud specifies that there is a regression to a cannibalistic mode of experience, and that introjection is rooted in the oral phase, he does not in fact relate melancholia to a regression to an infantile fixation point.

Abraham devoted much of his work to manic-depressive states and provides rich clinical material. Unlike Freud, he traces melancholia to its infantile roots and seeks in childhood its points of fixation. In his paper "A Short Study of the Development of the Libido, Viewed in the Light of Mental Disorders" (1924)[10] (see introduction) he subdivides Freud's libidinal stages. He places the fixation point of melancholia in the late-oral and early-anal stage. In that stage the object is devoured in phantasy, changed into feces, and expelled. The original object of this activity is the part object, the breast, though it could be extended to the mother as a whole. Abraham differs from Freud at that point, attributing to the relationship to the mother primary importance in depressive states. Freud speaks of introjection as based on primitive phantasies of cannibalistic incorporation, but the introjections he describes are in the Oedipal context. Abraham was the first to see the importance of those phantasies

[10] *Selected Papers of Karl Abraham*, pp. 418–501.

in the oral phase itself and the connection between anal expulsion and loss of internal objects. Unlike Freud, he thinks that normal mourning has similar elements. According to Abraham, in mourning the object is also introjected, but the difference is that the relation to the lost object contains more love and less hate than is the case in melancholia. He assumed that there is a "primary depression" in infancy to which both the melancholic and the mourner regress. Both Freud and Abraham relate mania to the depression, seeing it as a defense. Freud emphasizes the triumph over the devoured object in mania, Abraham emphasizes idealization: while in melancholia "the shadow of the object" fell upon the ego,[11] in mania "the bright radiance"[12] of the object falls on the ego.

Abraham established a further connection—between melancholia and obsessional neurosis. The fixation point of melancholia is in the second oral and first anal stage, in which the object is devoured, destroyed, and expelled. In the second anal stage concern for the object develops, and retention of the object is a defense against its destruction and loss. The obsessional patient suffers from the original ambivalence with its threat of the loss of the object, and mobilizes defenses against such a loss and the resulting depression. Abraham dates the beginning of the object relationship to that stage. Both Freud and Abraham put in evidence the narcissistic aspect of melancholia, but this narcissism is, at least in part, a secondary narcissism resulting from a relation to an internalized object. In Abraham's work one can see the beginning of a shift in emphasis. The relation to the object, even to the part object, assumes a greater importance. Though he agrees with Freud that the infant

[11] "Mourning and Melancholia," *SE* XIV, p. 249.
[12] Ibid., p. 442.

is narcissistic, and says that the object relation does not begin until the second anal stage, he does in fact describe a part-object relation existing earlier. He says that toward a part object there is a partial love. One may also assume that he saw the anal preoccupations of the first and second anal phase as being due not only to the emergence of the anus as the leading erogenous zone, which would dictate the nature of the object relationship, but also to the anxieties arising out of the object relationship—the wish to expel the object, then the wish to retain it. Those anxieties may dictate the increasing interest in and cathexis of the anal functions.

By 1923 Abraham and Klein must already have exerted a mutual influence on each other's thinking. Abraham, in a letter to Freud, says:

> I have assumed the presence of an early depression in infancy as the prototype of later melancholia. In the last few months Mrs Klein has skilfully conducted the psychoanalysis of a three-year-old with good therapeutic results. This child presented a true picture of the basic depression that I postulated in close combination with oral erotism. The case offered amazing insight into the infantile instinctual life.[13]

Klein's concept of the depressive position is obviously an extension of Abraham's "primal depression," but she develops it considerably. She places object relationships much earlier than Abraham, who considered the oral and anal stages to be primarily narcissistic. She follows Abraham's differentiation between part-object and whole-object relationships, but gives them an entirely new emphasis. She correlates the coming into being of a whole object with the experience of ambivalence, and the onset of depressive anxieties. But most significantly, perhaps,

[13] *A Psycho-Analytic Dialogue: The Letters of Sigmund Freud and Karl Abraham, 1906–27*, p. 339. Letter from Abraham to Freud of 7 October 1923.

by attaching even more importance than did Abraham to the fact that the depressive position is a universal phenomenon, she was able to study it not only in relation to pathological but also to normal development.

It is difficult to overestimate the importance of the introduction of the concept of the depressive position. Klein's work before that paper had described with great richness various anxiety situations, phantasies, and defenses in the child's development. Reading *The Psycho-Analysis of Children,* one can almost feel she describes too many phantasies, too many defenses. The depressive position brings into focus the problems. It is the task of the child in the course of development to establish securely in the core of his ego a good breast, mother, father, and a creative parental couple. The establishment of such introjects implies the great pain of working through the depressive position; the pain and internal danger situations that it involves lead to the formation of a cluster of defenses, which are described in such detail in Klein's casework, defending against the depressive position and impeding its development. The concept of the depressive position also enables her to differentiate more clearly between the psychotic and neurotic pathologies and points of fixation, as well as opening the way to the study of mourning and reparation and normal creative processes. The full implications, however, of the whole concept of positions do not become clear until the next step in her theoretical development when she introduces the paranoid/schizoid position.

• • •
VIII

Melanie Klein's presentation of her newest findings aroused considerable opposition. In the mid-
1930s both the atmosphere and the composition
of the British Psychoanalytical Society were
changing. Up to the time when she read in the
Society her paper on the psychogenesis of manic-
depressive states, one could not speak of a Kleinian school as distinct from the English school of
psychoanalysis as a whole. This, however, began
to change in 1935 when she introduced the concept of the depressive position. To begin with,
Edward Glover, who had been one of her most
enthusiastic supporters, radically changed his
views, accusing her of being nonanalytic and
contending that as a lay person she did not have
the psychiatric experience to entitle her to discuss
psychosis. Melitta Schmideberg, who became his
analysand, joined him in this attack. In the later

1930s many psychoanalysts, fleeing the Nazis, came to London from Berlin and even more from Vienna, among them, in 1938, Sigmund Freud and his family.

The controversy between Miss Freud and Mrs. Klein became the focus of the scientific life of the Society. There were increasing disagreements and implicit or explicit accusations that Klein's work was not consistent with Freud's. Ernest Jones and other old members of the British Society took Klein's side. Even if they did not agree with her views, they felt that her work was truly psychoanalytic, and that she had every right to hold her views and present them in the Psychoanalytical Society.

It was clear that the time was approaching for a serious debate of the issues. War, however, supervened and since many members of the Society were either called up or left London, it was decided to postpone discussion until a more auspicious time. Melanie Klein, among others, left London in 1939. Her son Eric joined the army, leaving his young wife, Judy, and their first baby, Michael. Melanie Klein went with Judy and Michael, first for a few months to Cambridge, and then to Pitlochry in Scotland, where she stayed for a little over a year and continued some of her work, including the analysis of Dick, the autistic boy who by now had reached puberty. She also analyzed for four months the ten-year-old Richard. This analysis was very important in the development of her work. It clarified for her the relations between the depressive position and the Oedipus complex and it is largely the material from this analysis that she used in her paper "The Oedipus Complex in the Light of Early Anxieties" (1945),[1] in which she revises her earlier views on the Oedipus complex. She had always longed to give a full account of the analysis of a child so that her technique, her work, and her theoretical conclusions could be dis-

[1] *Writings* I, pp. 370–419.

cussed on the basis of actual detailed material. In Pitlochry she could devote herself to the task of keeping
daily detailed notes of Richard's sessions immediately
after they occurred. She was not, however, able to publish
them in book form until the end of her life. By 1942,
when she went back to London, the life of the Society
was returning to normal. The old controversies were as
alive as ever. Ernest Jones, the president of the Society,
decided in 1943 to initiate a series of scientific discussions
on controversial issues. Later, in his introduction to
Melanie Klein's *Contributions to Psycho-Analysis* (*1921–
1945*),[2] he summarized the controversy as follows:

> The division in the British Society will, presently, I
> doubt not, be reproduced in all other psycho-analytical
> societies, and in the absence of colleagues with first-
> hand experience of Mrs Klein's work she must expect
> adverse critics to be in the majority. In England itself
> the storm was heightened by the advent of our Vien-
> nese colleagues whose life in their homeland had be-
> come literally impossible. They added to the other
> criticisms the opinion that Mrs Klein's conclusions not
> only diverged from but were incompatible with Freud's.
> This I find myself a grossly exaggerated statement.
> Not that it should be in any event a decisive considera-
> tion, if experience showed that her conclusions were
> nearer the truth; I yield to no one in my admiration of
> Freud's genius, but on several occasions I have not
> hesitated to put forward reasons for thinking that cer-
> tain of his inferences were imperfect. We had, how-
> ever, become so accustomed to regard on good grounds,
> various analysts who had separated from Freud, such
> as Adler, Jung, Stekel and Rank, as being influenced
> by subjective motives—a rationalization of inner re-
> sistances—rather than by a profounder insight, that
> it seemed to many less presumptuous, and certainly

2 London, 1948. Later republished as *Writings* I: *Love, Guilt
and Reparation and Other Works 1921–1945*. E. Jones's introduction is published as an Appendix to *Writings* III, pp. 337–
40.

easier, to place Mrs Klein in the same class. Yet, if psycho-analysis is to remain a branch of science it is evident that, now that Freud's ability to continue his magnificent impetus has been extinguished, advance beyond the limits he reached is inevitable.[3]

Nevertheless some of Mrs Klein's more abstract formulations will no doubt be modified in the future theoretic structure of psycho-analysis. What seems to me a probable example of this is her literal application to clinical findings of Freud's philosophical concept of a "death-impulse," about which I have serious misgivings. I quote it not for this reason, however, but because I find it a little odd that I should be criticizing her for a too faithful adherence to Freud's views, and odder still that certain Viennese analysts see in it a divergence from his views. All of which shows that psychoanalytical theorizing continues to be a very lively activity. And in this activity Mrs Klein's work is playing, and is likely to play, a very central part.[4]

These discussions, which came to be known as "Controversial Discussions," occupied the Society in 1943 and 1944. The basis for them was provided by four main papers, aiming at clarifying Melanie Klein's views. They were: "On the Nature and Function of Phantasy" by Susan Isaacs, "Some Aspects of the Role of Introjection and Projection" by Paula Heimann, "Regression" by Susan Isaacs and Paula Heimann, and "The Emotional Life and Ego Development of the Infant with Special Reference to the Depressive Position" by Melanie Klein. These papers, as well as all contributions to the discussion, were duplicated and are in the keeping of the British Psychoanalytical Society. The first three were published in 1952, together with a general introduction by Joan Riviere and a few other papers, in *Developments in Psycho-Analysis*. Klein, however, who by that time had elaborated further

[3] *Writings* III, pp. 337–38.
[4] Ibid., p. 340.

her thinking, contributed instead of the original paper three others which include her later views—namely: "Notes on some Schizoid Mechanisms," "Some Theoretical Conclusions regarding the Emotional Life of the Infant," and "On the Theory of Anxiety and Guilt."

The four major papers aimed at clarifying Klein's position in relation to Freud's metapsychology. Klein, throughout her writings, refers to Freud and indicates where she believes that she departs from his views. She differs from him, for instance, on the dating of the Oedipus complex and the beginning of the superego, the formation of the superego, the view of female sexuality, and on a number of other points; but she did not in any general way elaborate how her findings affect the broader metapsychological theory. The authors of the papers wished to refute the accusation that Melanie Klein departed from basic psychoanalytical views about the nature of psychic conflicts, anxieties, and defenses, but they also wanted to demonstrate how, grounded in Freud's theory, she nevertheless reaches certain conclusions differing from his. Freud started many trends of thought and did not, of course, develop all of them. Sometimes his views seem contradictory; for instance, he described the long development from auto-erotism via narcissism to object relationship, and yet referred frequently to the fact that the infant's first object is his mother's breast, speaking of introjection and projection as rooted in the earliest oral relationship; "I will take this in; I will spit that out."[5] Similarly, he sees the formation of the superego as part of the Oedipus complex at the age of three to five, and yet refers to earlier parental introjects and to regressive cannibalistic phantasies.

Joan Riviere begins her introduction to *Developments in Psycho-Analysis* by a quotation from Freud's *Autobiography*:

[5] "Negation" (1925), *SE* XIX.

. . . I have made many beginnings and thrown out many suggestions. I can hope that they have opened up a path to an important advance in our knowledge. Something will come of them in the future.[6]

Both sides of the controversy quoted Freud repeatedly, but the quotations were different. One could say, Which Freud? Whose Freud? Riviere remarks that Klein's opponents tended to refer to Freud's early work, while she and her co-workers referred more often to his later work. This is particularly clear in relation to the death instinct. The "Freudians" contended that the theory of the death instinct was, as one of the discussants put it, "a purely biological theory in which psychological conceptions so far have no place," but the Kleinians quoted such works as "The Economic Problem of Masochism" (1924)[7] and "Negation" (1925),[8] and referred to Freud's views that masochism and suicidal depression are directly derived from the death instinct. Riviere quotes from "The Ego and the Id":

> Defusion and a marked emergence of the death instinct are amongst the most noteworthy effects of many severe neuroses, e.g. the obsessional neuroses. . . . The essence of the regression of libido, e.g. from the genital to the sadistic anal level, would lie in a defusion of instincts, just as an advance from an earlier to the definitive genital phase would be conditioned by an accession of erotic components.[9]

Susan Isaacs's paper on phantasy, the first in the controversial discussion, is very important in illuminating Melanie Klein's views. It was read first, because it had become clear to all that to grasp Klein's views on the

[6] *Developments in Psycho-Analysis,* ed. J. Riviere, General Introduction, p. 1. The quotations from Freud in this work are not taken from *SE* but from an earlier translation.
[7] *SE* XIX.
[8] Idem.
[9] *Developments in Psycho-Analysis,* pp. 9–10.

early development of the ego and superego and the importance she attaches to the internal objects, it is essential to understand the use she makes of the concept of unconscious phantasy.

Isaacs relates Klein's views to those of Freud. Freud made scant use of the concept of unconscious phantasy, and where he refers to it explicitly, he considers it as a rather late phenomenon. In "Formulations Regarding the Two Principles of Mental Functioning" (1911) he says:

> With the introduction of the reality principle one species of thought activity was split off; it was kept free from reality-testing and remained subordinated to the pleasure principle alone.[10]

Differing on this point from Freud, Klein nevertheless bases her view of phantasy on his discovery of dynamic psychic reality:

> Freud's discovery of *dynamic psychical reality* initiated a new epoch of psychical understanding.
>
> He showed that the inner world of the mind has a continuous living reality of its own, with its own dynamic laws and characteristics, different from those of the external world. In order to understand the dream and the dreamer, his psychological history, his neurotic symptoms or his normal interests and character, we have to give up that prejudice in favour of external reality, and of our conscious orientations to it, that under-valuation of internal reality which is the attitude of the ego in ordinary civilized life today.[11]

Isaacs examines phantasy in relation to instincts, mental mechanisms, external reality, and higher mental functions. Phantasy springs from instincts. She quotes from Freud's "New Introductory Lectures on Psycho-Analysis" (1933): "We suppose that it (the id) is somewhere in

[10] *SE* XII, p. 222.
[11] "The Nature and Function of Phantasy," *Developments in Psycho-Analysis*, pp. 81–82.

direct contact with the somatic processes and takes over from the instinctual forces and gives them mental expression."[12] In his view instinct can only be perceived by its mental representative. Isaacs, at the same time presenting Melanie Klein's ideas, considers that unconscious phantasy is this mental expression of instincts: "All impulses, all feelings, all modes of defence are experienced in phantasy, which gives them mental life and shows their direction and purpose."[13] This is in keeping with the omnipotence which is the ruling characteristic of the infant's mind. Freud's assumption of a hallucinatory wish-fulfilment characteristic of the early stages of mental development would be consistent with her view.

> Let us consider further what Freud has to say about this situation.
> He goes on: "In so far as it is auto-erotic, the ego has no need of the outside world, but . . . it cannot but for a time perceive instinctual stimuli as painful. Under the sway of the preasure principle, there now takes place a further development. The objects presenting themselves, in so far as they are sources of pleasure, are absorbed by the ego into itself, 'introjected' (according to an expression coined by Ferenczi): while, on the other hand, the ego thrusts forth upon the external world whatever within itself gives rise to pain (*v. infra:* the mechanism of projection)."[14]
> Although in describing introjection, Freud does not use the phrase "unconscious phantasy," it is clear that his concept accords with our assumption of the activity of unconscious phantasy in the earliest phase of life.[15]

Freud's hypothesis of hallucinatory wish-fulfilment preceded that concerning the duality of life and death instincts and referred only to libidinal satisfactions.

[12] Ibid., p. 83.
[13] Idem.
[14] Ibid., pp. 86–87; "Instincts and Their Vicissitudes," (1915).
[15] "The Nature and Function of Phantasy," op. cit., pp. 86–87.

Susan Isaacs brings this idea up to date by drawing attention to the fact that destructive impulses also express themselves in phantasies, giving rise to anxiety and dread of persecution. In the omnipotent mind of the infant the desire to eat becomes an omnipotent phantasy of having incorporated an ideal nourishing breast. The desire to destroy becomes a phantasy of a destroyed and persecuting breast.

The earliest phantasies, of course, are nonverbal, and the nature of the phantasy will be dictated by the stage of the infant's development. To begin with they will be bodily, later visual, and finally verbalizable. Sometimes, however, the earliest phantasies can be expressed verbally at a later stage of development. Isaacs quotes an observation of Ernest Jones, who reported how a small boy, seeing his mother's nipple when she was feeding a younger sibling, said: "That is what you bit me with."[16] And she gives a similar example of a little girl with poor speech development who, at the age of one year and eight months, was terrified of her mother's shoe in which the sole had come loose. The shoes were removed, but fifteen months later when she could speak, she asked where they were and commented: "They might have eaten me right up."[17]

The earliest phantasies are oral and concerned with the incorporation and evacuation of objects and parts of the self. These phantasies are the basis of the earliest ego mechanisms—introjection and projection. The link between oral phantasies of incorporation and the processes of introjection had been discussed by Freud in a number of papers. Isaacs refers to his essay on "Negation" (1925);[18] speaking of the instinctual basis of what later becomes judgment, she writes:

[16] Ibid., p. 88.
[17] Ibid., p. 90.
[18] SE XIX.

Freud says: "Expressed in the language of the oldest, that is of the oral instinctual impulses, the alternative runs thus: 'I should like to take this into me and keep that out of me.' That is to say, it is to be either *inside me* or outside me." The wish thus formulated is the same thing as a phantasy.

What Freud picturesquely calls here "the language of the oral impulse," he elsewhere calls the "mental expression" of an instinct, *i.e.* the phantasies which are the psychic representatives of a bodily aim. In this actual example, Freud is showing us the phantasy that is the mental equivalent of an *instinct*. But he is at one and the same time formulating the subjective aspect of the *mechanism* of introjection (or projection). Thus *phantasy is the link between the id impulse and the ego mechanism,* the means by which the one is transmuted into the other. "I want to eat that and therefore I have eaten it" is a phantasy which represents the id impulse in the psychic life; it is at the same time the subjective experiencing of the mechanism or function of introjection.[19]

What applies to introjection and projection applies equally to other mechanisms of defense. Isaacs says that "mechanism" is an abstract description which we can use in theoretical formulations, but subjectively the infant or the patient is doing something in phantasy, splitting his object or himself, taking the objects in, pushing them out, isolating parts of himself, and so on. Thus phantasy is the link between instincts and mental mechanisms. Freud spoke of symptoms and dreams as achieving a compromise between the impulse and the defenses against it. The concept of unconscious phantasy as used by Isaacs encompasses this idea. A dream thought expresses an unconscious phantasy including instinctual and defensive elements. For instance, the phantasy of incorporating an object fulfills the oral instinctual aim and also serves defensive functions such as, for instance, defending against rage toward the absent object.

[19] "The Nature and Function of Phantasy," op. cit., p. 104.

But phantasy, of course, does not exist in a void. From the beginning of life the infant experiences reality. As Freud has made clear in many of his writings, the infant is never wholly under the sway of the pleasure-pain principle, or he would not survive. From the beginning of life phantasies are shaped and molded by reality; there is a constant interaction between the two. The infant's libidinal phantasy of a good all-feeding breast is reinforced by good experiences, while bad experiences reinforce his phantasies of a bad and persecuting object and the omnipotence of his own bad feelings. On the other hand, phantasy may override reality and the infant under the sway of persecutory anxieties may turn away angrily and in fear from the approaching breast, as is well known from observations of the infant's feeding difficulties. Only very gradually with the growth of the ego and reality-testing is phantasy differentiated from reality.

But phantasy life continues in the unconscious and provides the matrix from which higher mental functions such as thinking are evolved. Isaacs quotes from Freud's "Interpretation of Dreams": "Everything conscious has a preliminary unconscious stage."[20] This preliminary unconscious stage is an unconscious phantasy, and the link to the external world is made through symbolism. In finding symbolic expression for his unconscious phantasy in the external world, the child learns to explore the external world and relate to it, as Klein demonstrated in her work, and described in such papers as "The Role of the School in the Libidinal Development of the Child" (1923)[21] and "The Importance of Symbol-Formation in the Development of the Ego" (1930).[22] In this process the

[20] Ibid., p. 82.
[21] *Writings* I, pp. 59–76.
[22] Ibid., pp. 219–32.

phantasies can also be reality-tested. Freud said that the reality principle is nothing but the pleasure-pain principle altered by reality-testing. One could summarize Isaacs's view on higher mental functions by saying that thinking evolves out of unconscious phantasy through reality-testing.

One could regard the extension of the concept of unconscious phantasy as purely a verbal matter, in which what Freud called "psychic reality" is now called "phantasy." There are a number of Freud's concepts which fall under this extended term. For instance, is a hallucinatory wish-fulfilment, or are children's sexual theories, when these are unconscious, to be considered as unconscious phantasies? Indeed, in the Controversial Discussions, W. R. D. Fairbairn suggested that "psychic reality" could cover the phenomena described by Susan Isaacs. Marjorie Brierly suggested the term "unconscious meaning." But the problem is not merely verbal. The Kleinian approach to phantasy as presented by Susan Isaacs is linked with the view that there is enough ego at birth to form rudimentary object relationships and use primitive mental mechanisms such as projection, introjection, and splitting. Phantasy is not considered by Klein and Isaacs as a pure id phenomenon, but as an elaboration by the ego of impulses, defenses, and object relationships.

The second paper in the series—Paula Heimann's "Certain Functions of Introjection and Projection in Early Infancy"[23]—deals explicitly with the early ego and object relationships. She is particularly concerned with the role played by introjection and projection in the formation of both the ego and the superego. Ferenczi considered that introjection underlies all relation to reality. Freud first used the term in his paper on melancholia, in which he describes an ambivalently introjected object as the

[23] *Developments in Psycho-Analysis*, pp. 122–68.

center of the internal conflicts. He assumed that this introjection happened as part of a regression to a cannibalistic stage of development. Later on he based his description of the superego on the mechanism of introjection—the introjection of the father as a superego, leading to the resolution of the Oedipus complex—but never quite connected this later introjection with earlier ones, though he does refer occasionally to "earlier identifications with parents" before the Oedipus complex. He often uses interchangeably the terms "identification" and "introjection."

Paula Heimann presents Klein's view that introjection and projection are fundamental mental mechanisms existing from birth and continuing throughout life. The infant, from the beginning of life, introjects the desired breast, both in phantasy and in real feeding, and, desiring its goodness, identifies with this introject. This introjection is not only a function of the ego but an important root of its formation. The introjection of the original object is the basis of both the ego and the superego. This view is consistent with Freud's statement, in "The Ego and the Id," that one can only give up an object of desire by introjecting it and storing it in the ego. The difference lies in the importance Klein attaches to the early introjections, starting with the part object, the breast, and, as the infant develops, extending to other objects including the parents in the Oedipal situation. The question remains: if the breast and later objects are introjected in a way that promotes the growth of the ego as well as the superego, what determines when the object becomes part of the one or of the other? This, according to Heimann, depends on the emotional situation governing introjection. She differentiates between introjection and introjective identification. If the object is introjected mainly with the aim of identification it will become introjected into the ego and identified with. Such identifications apply, for instance, to the parents' admired skills. If the object is introjected in a situation of emotional conflict it is more likely to be introjected into the superego. In this paper, Heimann refers to all introjected objects as the superego, but she emphasizes that the many and various functions of the internal objects may not only be punishing but also be helpful, nourishing, and life-enhancing.

Originally Klein also referred to all introjects as the superego. In her later work, however, she speaks more frequently of "internal objects." These objects have many functions, according to the whole context of the introjection and the nature of the objects as well as the feelings with which they were introjected. They may be experienced as, for instance, feeding, helping, reinforcing sexuality, or, on the contrary, as persecuting and internally attacking the ego. One could think of the superego as that object, or that particular synthesis of various objects, which exercises moral pressure. Klein, however, is not consistent in her use of the term, sometimes making it synonymous with "internal object," sometimes referring only to that aspect of the object which exercises a superego function.

Projection plays an equally important role in early development. This is also implied in Freud's view of early mental functioning: "The objects presenting themselves in so far as they are sources of pleasure, are absorbed by the ego into itself, 'introjected' (according to the expression coined by Ferenczi); while, on the other hand, the ego thrusts forth upon the external world whatever within itself gives rise to pain."[24] But despite this statement, Freud generally considered projection as a late mechanism specific to paranoia; this "thrusting out of

[24] "Instincts and Their Vicissitudes" (see *SE* XIV, p. 136, and n. 6 above).

itself" is, in fact, a projection of parts of the self into the outside world, since the pain within "is due to one's own mental functioning." A projection does not involve only destructive feelings and objects. The libido is also projected on to the good object, meeting it halfway, and it is this projection of the infant's own good feelings which idealizes the experience and creates the ideal breast. But, in the main, the infant's aim is to get rid of the bad and to internalize the good. In favorable circumstances the projected badness is mitigated by good real experiences, while goodness is increased. This is the basis of a strong ego and a helpful internal object—the foundation of mental health.

The early introjections are wholly egocentric. The "good" is good for me, the "bad" is bad for me. This egocentricity diminishes in the depressive position, but the processes of introjection continue, only the introjections are now related increasingly to parents as real people and the introjection is dominated by the Oedipus complex. Paula Heimann emphasizes the projective aspects of the Oedipus complex. Children attribute to the parents' sexual activities their own sexual phantasies.

The importance claimed by Melanie Klein for introjection and projection and for early object relations is at variance with Freud's views. Broadly speaking, he considers that the infant is, to begin with, auto-erotic (that is, concerned with sensations without an object), then narcissistic (taking himself for an object), and finally object-oriented (seeking an erotic object in his mother). At the same time, however, Freud does not exclude the existence of an object relation from the beginning. Heimann quotes from the first of his two Encyclopaedia articles of 1922:

> In the first instance the oral component instinct finds satisfaction "anaclitically" by attaching itself to the

sating of the desire for nourishment; and its object is the mother's breast. It then detaches iself, becomes independent and at the same time *auto-erotic,* that is, finds an object in the child's own body. Others of the component instincts start by being auto-erotic and are not diverted till later on to an external object. . . .[25]

But though Freud sometimes refers to the breast as the infant's first object, it is the auto-erotic and narcissistic development that he emphasizes. Heimann links auto-erotism and narcissism with object relations by using the concept of phantasy and introjection. It is by introjecting a good breast in phantasy that the infant can become auto-erotic. If the infant can give up the breast and turn, say, to sucking his own thumb, it is by virtue of having introjected the breast and of identifying the thumb with it. This view is in keeping in fact with Freud's own view that introjection may be "the sole condition on which an object can be given up."[26] In an auto-erotic state the infant has successfully introjected a good breast and projected both the bad object and the bad feelings. In narcissism the situation is more complicated. Narcissism is a later condition, more hostile to the external world and involving a greater perception of frustration. The hallucinatory wish-fulfilment is less successful and the turning against a bad external object is more in evidence than the turning to a good internal one. Thus, narcissism plays an important part in such severe forms of mental illness as paranoia. Melanie Klein was to extend this view of narcissism in her later work.

The important contention of Heimann's paper is that auto-erotism and narcissism are ways of dealing with

---

[25] *Developments in Psycho-Analysis,* p. 140 (see *SE* XVIII, p. 245, and n. 6 above).
[26] Ibid., p. 145. See "Mourning and Melancholia," *SE* XIV; "The Ego and the Id," *SE* XIX; "New Introductory Lectures," *SE* XXII; etc.

frustration and are linked with phantasies about internal and external objects. The auto-erotic and narcissistic, purely egocentric object relations gradually give way to more mature object relationships, but projection and introjection continue throughout life.

The third paper in the series, written jointly by Paula Heimann and Susan Isaacs on the theme of regression, takes up again the theme of phantasy and early object relationships. Regression is seen by Freud as the principal mechanism ushering in mental illness. It is intimately related to the idea of fixation. In psychosexual development, for biological reasons, the libido progresses from the oral to the anal and urethral and finally to the genital phase. The earlier aims are never completely abandoned, but when genital primacy is established, they become subordinate to the genital. At any point in development, however, libido may become fixated at a pre-genital zone. Such fixations not only result in the retention of a pre-genital sexual aim; they also affect the whole personality. They may result in inhibitions as well as in perversions and may affect character structure. The fixation is due to what Freud describes as the damming up of the libido so that, while some libidinal development continues, a large quantity of the libido may remain fixated to the earlier aim and object. Freud relates such fixations to frustration, whether it is due to external or internal factors.

Isaacs and Heimann make the point that this theory of regression precedes Freud's views on the duality of instincts, and does not take into account the role of aggression. Freud observed regression to the various points of fixation in his analysis of adults. In her work with children, Melanie Klein was able to observe at the time of their occurrence how such fixation points are formed. In her view, it is aggression and anxiety which produce the fixation. From the beginning of life there is a conflict between aggressive and libidinal impulses, in which gradually the libidinal forces master aggression and anxiety. In genital sexuality, which is creative and procreative, aggression is put at the service of the libidinal aim. At any point of development in which aggression and anxiety become excessive, libido is also fixated to overcome the anxiety. This directly contradicts Freud in representing the fixation of the libido not as the cause but as the effect of the pathological process.

Freud's theory of fixation and regression of the libido does not take into account object relations. Isaacs and Heimann contend that one cannot understand the processes of fixation and regression in isolation from the object relations, the phantasy life, and the anxiety due to aggression. They give as one example oral fixation in the drug addict. In this case, early cannibalistic phantasies give rise to anxiety, guilt, and depression, which have to be constantly allayed and reassured by ever renewed oral gratifications. Thus an oral fixation of the libido is due to anxiety and guilt.

Situations of guilt and anxiety due to aggression are part of normal development. Melanie Klein often shows in her work with children that anxiety can be a spur to development, to reparative phantasies, and a movement of the libido to higher levels of organization. Whether it will lead to a fixation or to progress depends on the degree of anxiety. When the anxiety cannot be mastered, a vicious circle results. Large amounts of libido have to be immobilized at the pre-genital level to counteract the anxiety. This results in a weak genital organization and a poorer capacity to withstand frustration; therefore regression easily occurs.

But the entire concept of regression is seen somewhat differently to Klein and her co-workers. For them the pre-genital stages play a far more important role in the genital organization than was assumed by Freud. In clinical work they do not consider the appearance of pre-genital material as being necessarily evidence of regression. The early oral introjections of the good breast and the good penis are the basis of good genitality, and the genital act contains all the symbolism of good mutual feeding. Furthermore, the guilt of the early attacks on the breast, the mother's body, and the parental intercourse give rise to reparative wishes which find their expression in full genitality. When regression occurs it is never simply due to frustration. It is the breakdown of the effectiveness of reparation which mobilizes more primitive forms of guilt and anxiety and leads to regression; and not only does the libido regress, but there is a regression to more primitive, more destructive, and more anxiety-ridden internal and external object relations.

They say:

> While some analysts think of regression predominantly in terms of the libido, we see *concurrent* changes in the destructive impulses as well, *i.e.* they return to earlier, archaic aims. We hold that it is this *recurrence of primitive destructive aims which is the chief causative factor in the outbreak of mental illness.*[27]

It is always the failure of the libido to master the aggressive components which leads to illness.

Generally speaking, Heimann and Isaacs see the pre-genital and the genital stages as being much more interconnected. Melanie Klein contended both that the genital trends appear already in the oral stage and that the pre-genital components play a large part in the genital organization, and the authors of this paper make the point that there is a constant movement to and fro, the prime mover of which is anxiety.

[27] P. Heimann and S. Isaacs, "Regression," *Developments in Psycho-Analysis*, p. 186.

A few years later, when Klein came to formulate her theory of the paranoid-schizoid position, the concepts of fixation points and regression lost much of their importance for her, as she came to look at the mental structure in a slightly different way.

The last paper in the series was Klein's "The Emotional Life of the Infant, with Special Emphasis on Depressive Anxieties." Here she restates her views on child development and the central role of the depressive position, correlating them more closely with those of Freud and Abraham. In particular, she draws attention to Freud's later thinking about guilt, when he links it specifically with aggression. She quotes from "Civilization and Its Discontents" (1930):

> . . . *it is after all only the aggression which is changed into guilt,* by being suppressed and made over to the superego. I am convinced that very many processes will admit of much simpler and clearer explanation if we restrict the findings of psycho-analysis in respect of the origin of the sense of guilt to the aggressive instincts.[28] [Klein's italics.]

She remarks, however, that Freud has not altered his view that guilt appears at the time of the Oedipus complex and is specifically linked with it. Abraham, on the other hand, sees the origin of guilt in the cannibalistic phantasies of the oral phase—a view consistent with her own observations in child analysis. She comments that, while Abraham's work on the oral and anal phase had never been contested, neither had it been fully accepted and integrated into contemporary psychoanalytical thought, excepting her own and her co-workers'. She restates in the paper her views on the early object relationships and the origin of anxiety and guilt in the aggres-

---

[28] M. Klein, "On the Theory of Anxiety and Guilt," *Developments in Psycho-Analysis,* p. 273 (see *SE* XXI, p. 138, and n. 6 above).

sive component of unconscious phantasies. This paper, which she never published, made two new points. She added to her earlier views on symbolism a new element pertaining to the depressive position—namely, that it is not only anxiety but also concern for the object, love and guilt, which prompts the child partly to displace his interest from the original object and distribute it among symbolic representatives. She also gives a detailed examination of babies' and children's feeding difficulties in the light of cannibalistic impulses and the anxiety and guilt arising out of them.

The Controversial Discussions occupied the British Society from January 1943 until May 1944—with eleven meetings in all. The discussions did not bring, as Jones had hoped, a better mutual understanding. On the contrary, they seemed to have led to a still sharper polarization of views and sometimes degenerated into acrimony. From the scientific point of view, the useful result of the discussions was that they compelled Mrs. Klein and her co-workers to a more rigorous formulation of their views —Susan Isaacs's paper on phantasy can be singled out as a major theoretical contribution. The papers on introjection and projection, and on regression, made useful links between the classical theory and the Kleinian development. The discussion resulted in the clearer emergence of three distinct schools of thought: the followers of Anna Freud, those of Melanie Klein, and the majority, a large group of British analysts, prepared to accept some of Melanie Klein's findings, but not all. This scientific division led also to structural changes in the British Society. Glover resigned from the Society, and soon afterward Melitta and Walter Schmideberg left for the United States. Miss Freud and her group remained in the Society, but requested that their candidates have separate clinical seminars. A committee was formed under the chairmanship of Dr. Sylvia Payne to reorganize the training at the British Institute. The training analysts and their candidates were divided into two groups—the B Group (Anna Freud and her followers) and the A Group (the rest of the Society). The A Group comprised the Kleinians and what came to be known as the Middle Group, the uncommitted analysts. The administration of the Society was based on a gentleman's agreement, insuring that, by common consent, all groups would be equally represented on administering bodies. The candidates attended a common theoretical course, in which there was, in the third year, a course on Melanie Klein's work, but they attended separate clinical seminars. At present, candidates still have separate clinical seminars in their first and second year of training, but in the third year they come together in a combined seminar which is taken in turn by teachers of different technical orientations. The acrimony of the early controversies having died down, the training aims at giving the candidates not only a firm basis in their chosen technique but also an acquaintance with divergent points of view. Controversies in the psychoanalytical societies are often violent and embittered. This may be due to the emotionally highly charged subject matter and also to the unresolved transference feelings of psychoanalysts in relation to their training analysts. Only too often this results in societies and institutes splitting and personal conflicts become more important than the differences in the scientific outlook. The British Society has managed to weather the storm and to contain differing views. It became a forum in which scientific views could be discussed.

For Melanie Klein, the reorganization of the Society after the Controversial Discussions was on the whole a helpful development. She now had her own group of colleagues and candidates and could devote herself to fur·

ther scientific work and to training those who agreed
with her basic premises without having constantly to
defend her views. At the same time, the teaching of her
work in the third year of the training course and the
opportunity to present her work frequently in the Society,
as well as the increasing number of papers by her immediate colleagues and those trained by her, insured that
all the members of the Society had access to her work.
She made a point of never missing an International Congress and she read a paper at every Congress after 1919.

The Paranoid-Schizoid Position

•

IX

In 1946, two years after the Controversial Discussions, Melanie Klein wrote one of her most seminal papers, "Notes on Some Schizoid Mechanisms."[1] In her earlier work there was a certain contradiction; in various papers she had agreed with Abraham's view that there was a first oral pre-ambivalent stage and that aggression was mobilized in the oral sadistic stage. She had also spoken of the phase where sadism is at its height, corresponding to the second oral and first anal phase. Later she abandoned this formulation in favor of her concept of the depressive position where love and hatred come into acute conflict. Yet her stated agreement with Abraham's view was at variance both with her belief that the death instinct is operative from birth and with much of her clinical material.

[1] *Writings* III, pp. 1–24.

In her clinical material she often described very primitive part objects of an intensely persecutory nature, such as the "*Butzen*" of Rita[2] (see chapter iv, above, pages 42–43). In *The Psycho-Analysis of Children,* she writes about an adult male homosexual patient, Mr. B,[3] who had severe hypochondriacal anxieties and ideas of persecution and reference (delusions that everything has reference to oneself). For instance, when he was staying in a boarding-house, a slight gastric indisposition made him believe that he had been poisoned by a loaf of bread which a woman had bought for him. He also thought she was pursuing him sexually and plotting against his life. He hated and feared women's bodies because of their "sticking-out" parts—breasts and buttocks. In the analysis it appeared that his unconscious phantasy was that women's breasts and buttocks were so full of sadistic penises and excrement that they were bursting. He also had a frightening phantasy of breasts as harpies. Mrs. Klein traced these phantasies to a projection of his own intense sadism, oral at first—the breasts becoming harpies—and later anal and phallic. Split off from these bad part objects, he had a phantasy of an idealized penis, first represented by his pacifier and the bottle, then by the penis of an elder brother with whom he practiced fellatio. At that time Mrs. Klein thought that because of his oral frustration (he had never been breast-fed) he lacked a fixation at the first oral stage and so became fixated at the second sadistic one. But in "Personification in the Play of Children" (1929),[4] she states another point of view; she describes in detail the splitting between the ideal and persecutory objects which, she considers, is the basis of paranoia and she asserts that the more extreme such

[2] *Writings* II, p. 6.
[3] Ibid., pp. 264–78.
[4] *Writings* I, pp. 199–209.

splitting the more primitive the object relationship the earlier is the fixation point.

In "A Contribution to the Psychogenesis of Manic-Depressive States" (1935),[5] she makes a direct connection between splitting and part-object relationships, and states definitely that part-object relationships, splitting, and persecutory anxiety belong together and precede the depressive position in which integration begins to occur. The first clear statement of her disagreement with Abraham's view was made by Susan Isaacs and Paula Heimann in their paper on regression:

> Freud saw the first destructive aim arising during the primacy of the oral zone, namely cannibalism. Abraham subdivided the oral phase into oral-sucking and oral-biting stages. He pointed out the force of the destructive impulses during the onset of teething, but he held that the first oral stage was free from aggressive impulses. (*In this we do not follow him. . . .*)[6] [My italics.]

In the "Notes on Some Schizoid Mechanisms" (1946), she clarifies her views on infantile development preceding the depressive position. It is a phase of part-object relationships, and it is dominated by persecutory anxiety and schizoid mechanisms. Fairbairn[7] had used the term "schizoid position" to describe the original, split state of the primitive ego. Klein had emphasized the ideal and persecutory aspects of the early object relationship and called it originally "the paranoid position." In 1942 she introduced the term "paranoid-schizoid" to emphasize the coexistence of splitting and persecutory anxiety. To con-

[5] Ibid., pp. 262–89.
[6] P. Heimann and S. Isaacs, "Regression," *Developments in Psycho-Analysis*, p. 185.
[7] W. R. D. Fairbairn, "A Revised Psychopathology of the Psychoses and Psychoneuroses," *Int. J. Psycho-Anal.* 22 (1941); "Endopsychic Structure Considered in Terms of Object Relationships," *Int. J. Psycho-Anal.* 25 (1944).

ceptualize her many observations and her views of the early development she uses as a theoretical framework Freud's theory of the life and death instincts.

She differs from Freud on two points having to do with the nature of the early ego and primitive anxiety. Freud says that, threatened by the death instinct, the organism deflects it outward. He used the word "organism" rather than "ego" to emphasize that he considers it a biological and not yet a psychological entity. Klein, on the contrary, contends that there is enough ego at birth to experience anxiety and to use a defense mechanism. She does not speak of an organism deflecting, but of a primitive ego projecting the death instinct. Since the early ego, as she conceives it, is also capable of primitive phantasy object relationships, this projection therefore gives rise to a phantasy of a bad object: not deflection into a void but projection into an object.

This view of the early ego influences also her view of anxiety. Freud believes that the unconscious and the infant, and even the small child, have no idea of death, and that the fear of death is a derivative of castration anxiety. He therefore does not connect the death instinct directly with anxiety. Klein, thinking in terms of a primitive ego, maintains that the operation of the death instinct gives rise to a fear of annihilation, and that it is this basic fear which leads to the defensive projection of the death instinct. Thus she sees not an organism, a purely biological concept, deflecting the death instinct, but an ego projecting the death instinct as a defense against fear of annihilation.

Because this early ego is to begin with very weak and unintegrated, under the impact of anxiety it tends to fragment and to disintegrate. The terror of disintegration and total annihilation is the deepest fear stirred by the operation of the death instinct within.

From the beginning of life there is a struggle between the life and death instincts. Splitting, projection and introjection are the first mechanisms of defense. At the behest of the life instinct the ego splits off and projects the death instinct outward. At the same time the life instinct is partly projected in order to create an ideal object. In that way, out of chaos a primitive organization emerges. The ego splits into a libidinal and a destructive part and relates to a similarly split object.

The aim of the ego at that stage is to introject and identify with its ideal object and to keep at bay the persecutors, who also contain the projected destructive impulses. The central conflict between the life and death instincts becomes a struggle between the libidinal good self, identified and allied with the ideal object, and the persecutors. I put "persecutors" in the plural because, while the ideal object is felt to be whole and intact, the bad object is usually fragmented. This is so partly because it is a part of the ego fragmented by the death instinct which is projected, and partly because the oral sadism which expresses itself in biting leads to the hated object being perceived as bitten up into pieces. Urinary and anal sadism are soon added to the oral, so that the persecutors are imbued with sadism from all sources.

The leading anxiety at that stage is lest these persecutors destroy both the self and the ideal object, and against this anxiety schizoid mechanisms are used, such as increasing the split between the ideal and the bad object, and excessive idealization. Omnipotent denial is used as a defense against the fear of persecution. The phantasy underlying this mechanism is that of omnipotently annihilating the persecutors. Considered in this light, hallucinatory wish-fulfilment is not a simple phenomenon. To maintain a wish-fulfiling hallucination the infant must successfully maintain the idealization of his good object and omnipotently annihilate the bad. When he does not succeed and hunger sets in again, the experience is one of being invaded by persecutors and threatened by annihilation. At that primitive stage of development there is no experience of absence—the lack of the good object is felt as an attack by bad objects. The infant is gnawed by his hunger. Frustration is felt as a persecution. Good experiences merge with and reinforce the phantasy of an ideal object. Although the first oral phase is pre-ambivalent, this is not because hatred is not present but because there is a split between love and hate. Klein demonstrated in her material that the ideal relation to the breast which led Abraham to postulate a pre-ambivalent relationship does indeed exist, but she also observed, simultaneously and split off from it, a relation full of fear and hate to a very bad breast. Omnipotent denial, splitting, projection, and idealization had all been described before. The novelty of Klein's new formulation lies in her seeing their origin in the paranoid-schizoid position, and relating them to the most primitive relationship to the breast and to persecutory anxiety.

She introduces one new mechanism: that of projective identification. Projective identification evolves out of the primitive projection. In projective identification it is not the impulse only, but parts of the self (e.g., the baby's mouth and penis) and bodily products (e.g., his urine and feces) which are in phantasy projected into the object. In her clinical material Klein had often demonstrated the operation of this mechanism. For instance, in "The Importance of Symbol-Formation in the Development of the Ego"[8] (see chapter v above, page 64ff), she shows how Dick equates his sadism with his bad feces or penis, and it is these that are projected into his mother's body, which then becomes identified with those projected parts. In

[8] *Writings* I, pp. 219–32.

Mr. B's phantasy the breasts are identified with a greedy projected mouth and become harpies, or else they are bursting with bad penises and feces, projected parts of the child. In the phantasy of the harpies, the breast is completely identified with the projected mouth. In the case of the "sticking-out" bursting breast, it is phantasied as containing projected parts that are identified with a penis inside the breast. The breast is felt to be possessed and spoiled by them, but not completely identified with them. Klein had found this kind of phantasy so important that in the "Notes on Some Schizoid Mechanisms" she coins the term "projective identification." In describing it I have used interchangeably the terms "mechanism" and "phantasy." Susan Isaacs has shown how phantasy underlies ego mechanisms,[9] and this is most clear in the case of projective identification underlying the mechanism of projection. For Mr. B, breasts bite, penetrate, and soil, a projection of his own sadistic impulses. Underlying this projection there is the phantasy of his having actually projected his biting mouth, his piercing penis, his soiling feces, into them.

Not only parts, but the whole self, may in phantasy be projected into an object. Split off from phantasies about the mother's body full of projected parts and terrifying, Dick had also a phantasy of a mother whose inside was empty and into whom he could project himself wholly. He acted it out, hiding in an empty cupboard. In a later paper, "On Identification,"[10] Klein takes an example from literature, Julien Green's novel *If I Were You*,[11] to show how such a projection of the whole of oneself into another can lead to total identification, a taking over of the

---

[9] 'The Nature and Function of Phantasy," *Developments in Psycho-Analysis.*
[10] *Writings* III, pp. 141–75.
[11] London, 1930. Translated from the French by J. H. F. McEwen.

other's personality. The main character in Green's book, Fabian, hungry, depressed, and discontented with himself, enters by magic into other people and takes over their personalities. He then finds himself trapped in them. Such projective identifications underlie psychotic delusions of being another person: Christ, Napoleon, et al. The aim of the projection influences the resulting phantasy. In Dick the aim was to return to an empty womb out of fear. Fabian represents a phantasy of projective identification in the service of greedy and envious wishes to take over the position and personality of an object seen as enviable.

The aims of projective identification can be manifold: getting rid of an unwanted part of oneself, a greedy possession and scooping out of the object, control of the object, and so forth. One of the results is identification of the object with the projected part of the self (hence the term "projective identification"). Projection of bad parts leads to persecution. Yet projective identification involves not only parts of the self which are bad, but also those felt to be good. The good parts may be projected in order to avoid separation, in order to idealize the object, and also in order to avoid internal conflict; when the inside is felt to be full of badness, the good parts of the self may be projected into an ideal breast, given to the object for safe-keeping. This leads to excessive idealization of the object and the devaluation of the self.

Projective identification is the basis of narcissistic object relationships and of a narcissistic internal structure, since the object is also reintrojected. Klein differentiates between narcissistic states, which are states of identification with an internal ideal object (corresponding to what Freud described as auto-erotism), and the narcissistic structure and narcissistic object relationships which are based on projective identification. Freud had described the narcissistic object choice in which the subject seeks and loves himself in his partner. Klein describes the detailed phantasies on which such a choice is based and their consequences. When parts of the self are projected and the object is identified with them, there is a need to control the object, and a constant fear of being controlled by it. When bad parts are projected, the object becomes a dreaded persecutor; when good parts are projected, there is a particular schizoid dependence on the object: it has to be controlled, because the loss of the object would entail the loss of a part of oneself. At the same time there is a fear of being completely controlled, since the object contains a valued part of the self. The schizoid fear of loving is based on the fact that when projective identification is the leading mechanism, loving means projecting good parts of the self into the object, and therefore depleting oneself and feeling enslaved. Because of the dangers involved in object relationships based on projective identification, the schizoid person may seek to cut himself off from all object relationships. This accounts for the fact that it was thought for a long time that narcissistic and schizoid patients developed no transference. The reintrojection of such objects into whom massive projection has taken place gives rise to the narcissistic structure. The infant contains an object which is broken up and fragmented, controlled and controlling. To protect himself from such an object he flees to an excessively idealized internal object. This excessively idealized object is also excessively controlled and controlling, and the ego is so depleted by projections that it may become a mere shell for such internal objects.

The schizoid mechanisms, starting with the relation to the breast, continue to operate in relation to the mother's whole body. In her earlier work Klein had described how the mother's body becomes a source of terror at the time of the primitive Oedipus complex and the boy's feminine phase. She related it to the sadistic attacks the child makes in his phantasy (see chapter iv above). Looking back on this material one can see that the attacks described there are carried out by means of projective identification, so that the mother's body is phantasized as full of and identified with the child's projected parts. Projective identification and reintrojection in relation to the mother's body are of paramount importance. The paranoid fears she connected with that phase are a continuation of the paranoid-schizoid relation to the breast.

The paranoid-schizoid position is a developmental step. The infant overcomes his fear of disintegration by the introjection of and identification with the ideal breast. The original splitting is a first step in the capacity to differentiate, and projective identification the first step in relating to the external world. But when the anxiety in that phase is excessive, the unresolved problems give rise to the most severe pathology. The paranoid anxiety and schizoid defenses of that early phase of development underlie the schizophrenic group of illnesses, the schizoid personality, and the paranoid or schizoid features of infantile or adult neuroses.

The fear of total disintegration and annihilation is at the basis of schizophrenic and schizoid disorders. The schizoid patient appears often devoid of anxiety. Dick is an extreme example of that. But the latent anxiety is of a catastrophic nature. The schizoid defenses are deployed against this anxiety, but they in turn produce anxieties of their own. The initial projection of the death instinct gives rise to paranoid and hypochondriacal anxieties. The projection of good parts of the self produces depletion. The operation of projective identification again gives rise to specific anxieties: there is a fear of retaliation by the object projecting into the self, and this may block and prevent introjection. Since part of the self is projected into the object, there is a fear of being imprisoned and controlled. Delusions of thought control, for instance, are based on such a phantasy. Claustrophobia is based on similar fears. Fragmentation of the ego, splitting, and projection all weaken the ego. Omnipotent annihilation of the unwanted parts of the ego is even more damaging. Turning the aggression on oneself to get rid of the unwanted parts is a significant and dangerous schizoid mechanism of defense. When the ego is weakened by an excessive use of such defenses, the infant cannot cope with the new anxieties he has to face in the depressive position.

The "Notes on Some Schizoid Mechanisms" is relatively short (only twenty-three pages, not counting Mrs. Klein's comments on Freud's Schreber case,[12] which are an addendum) but it is extraordinarily compressed and rich. It has opened a new field of psychoanalytical investigation of the schizoid and schizophrenic type disorders. Melanie Klein's paper was shortly followed by a number of others written by her co-workers, and using the new insights into schizoid anxieties and mechanisms of defense to illuminate the problems of analyzing schizophrenics. Her description of projective identification, which occupies only a couple of pages in this paper, stimulated work which explores further, clarifies, and differentiates various forms of projective identification. When describing the pathology of the paranoid-schizoid position, Klein speaks of excessive anxiety and excessive use of defenses. Following her paper, a number of psychoanalysts treating psychotic and borderline cases began to elucidate further the roots of pathology in the paranoid-schizoid position, seeking to define the factors which lead

[12] "Psycho-Analytic Notes upon an Autobiographical Account of a Case of Paranoia (Dementia Paranoides)," *SE* XII.

to excessive anxiety and studying in detail the nature of the defenses. Projective identification, for instance, may not only be excessive, but may become pathological in its form.

The interplay between the paranoid-schizoid and the depressive position became a focus of attention.

New Light on the Structural Theory of Mind,
Anxiety, and Guilt

The concepts of the paranoid-schizoid and depressive positions enabled Melanie Klein to formulate
a coherent and comprehensive theory of psychological development and its pathology. In *The
Psycho-Analysis of Children* and her early papers,
though she was pursuing always the thread of
anxiety, and always analyzed in terms of object
relations, in her theory she tried to accord all her
findings with Freud's and Abraham's formulations
of the libidinal phases. The concept of positions
permits a new approach. The position is not com-
parable to a phase of the development of the
libido. True, the paranoid-schizoid position precedes the depressive position; nevertheless, the
constant fluctuations between the two positions
makes "position" a structural concept rather than
a chronological one. The term "position" refers to
a state of organization of the ego and describes

characteristically conjoint phenomena: the state of the ego, the nature of the internal object relationships, the nature of anxiety and characteristic defenses. The formulation of the positions enabled her also to clarify her views on the nature of anxiety and guilt.

She now describes the development of the child as a working through of the conflict between the life and death instincts, with the life instinct gradually prevailing over the destructive drives. In the paranoid-schizoid position projection of the death instinct gives rise to the fear of persecutors. When reintrojected these bad objects form the persecutory aspect of the superego. Simultaneously the life instinct, in search of a life-giving object, is also partly deflected, creating an ideal object. This ideal object is introjected and partly identified with, thus becoming the core of both the ego and the superego. The growth and development of the ego are bound up with the operation of the life instinct. In favorable development, when good experiences predominate, there is less pressure to project the bad impulses and objects outward. As projections diminish, the persecution lessens and a benevolent cycle sets in. The lessening of persecutory fears in turn diminishes aggression and, therefore, anxiety and the need to project. When this happens the split between the ideal and persecutory objects diminishes and the stage is set for an integration of the object and the ego, and for a gradual move to the depressive position. In the papers on the depressive position that precede the "Notes on Some Schizoid Mechanisms," Klein emphasizes the importance in that position of persecutory fears. Clinically and developmentally it is certainly true that persecutory anxieties persist in the depressive position. It is, however, useful to regard the two positions as theoretical concepts and to consider the persecutory fears still operative in the depressive position as belonging to the paranoid-schizoid position; the working through of the depressive position could then be considered precisely as the overcoming of the paranoid-schizoid elements by the depressive ones.

One could contrast the paranoid-schizoid and the depressive organization schematically in the following way: In the paranoid-schizoid position the ego is split into its good and bad parts. It is fragmented. It is often confused with the object in projective identification. In the depressive position the ego is integrated and exposed to the conflict of contradictory impulses. The relation to the object in the paranoid-schizoid position is wholly egocentric and omnipotent. The object is a part object, both in the sense of being not a person but an anatomical part, and in the sense of being split into ideal and persecutory objects. The paranoid-schizoid object relationships are mainly based on projective identification. When the objects are reintrojected, they become the ideal and persecutory roots of the superego. In the depressive position the objects are persons: mother, father, and eventually the parental couple. They are seen as whole objects, both in the sense of being persons, and in the sense of not being split into totally good and totally bad figures. The relation to the object is ambivalent and when it is introjected it becomes the depressive superego. This superego is a loved object, and attacks on it give rise to a sense of guilt. The leading anxiety in the paranoid-schizoid position has to do with the survival of the self. It is either the fear of the operation of the death instinct inwards—thus of self-destructiveness—or the fear of persecutors destroying the self and the ideal object. In the depressive position the anxiety concerns injury to and loss of the object through one's own aggression—the fear for the self is linked to the identification with the object.

Guilt appears in the depressive position as a sense of

personal responsibility about one's own aggression against the good object. However, in the early stages of the depressive position guilt may still be of a very persecutory nature. Thus an internal object attacked and injured in phantasy may be felt as vengeful if projections are still operative. The superego of the melancholic for instance is full of projections. Such a superego transitional between persecution and guilt gives rise to a most painful form of persecutory guilt. In remorse the bitten object bites back; there is both acknowledgment of one's responsibility and a feeling of persecution.

The depressive position starts in a setting of dependence—the infant's complete dependence on the mother —but with the internalization of good objects, as well as with physiological growth, the dependence gradually diminishes, and the diminution of dependence mitigates the hostile element in ambivalence and furthers anew the internalization of good objects. Similarly, the increasing confidence in one's own reparative capacities lessens the dependence on the external object, as well as lessening the need for defensive maneuvers. Looking at the infant's and child's development as an evolution from the paranoid-schizoid to the depressive position puts the phases of libidinal development into a different perspective. The concept of the two positions does not do away with the basic idea of a movement of the libidinal and destructive forces from the oral to the genital phase. Both positions are rooted in the oral phase, which is dictated by the infant's dependence on nourishment from the breast. The anal trends appear as not so sharply separated off from the oral. Expulsion and projection are basic primitive mechanisms, and expulsion can be phantasied either in oral terms (burping, spitting) or in urinary and anal terms (urinating, passing wind, defecating). The devoured and fragmented bad breast is equated with feces which have to be expelled or, in certain situations, idealized. In the depressive position, when the destroyed object is equated with the stool, a mixture of depressive and manic trends brings in an anxious preoccupation with the stool—the need sometimes to hold it back from a fear of loss, or the opposite need, to expel it. The manic control over the object is often linked with a phantasy of turning it into feces. Obsessional mechanisms evolve out of the need to control this fecal object, as both Abraham and Klein have observed. One could put it this way: in classical theory it appears that the child develops a certain kind of object relationship because he is fixated in the anal stage; the Kleinian view would be that because the child develops a certain type of object relationship, he may get fixated to anal mechanisms. The wish to be anally penetrated would be seen by Klein as a defensive displacement from the oral or genital trends, the anus representing an incorporating mouth or vagina.

In Klein's view, the Oedipus complex begins to emerge with, and is part and parcel of, the depressive position. The working through of the one is intimately bound up with the working through of the other. When the parents are seen as whole and real people, their relationship is also perceived, giving rise to Oedipal wishes and fears. To the early ambivalence in relation to the breast is added acute Oedipal rivalry and jealousy. The feelings of exclusion, frustration, jealousy, and envy are aggravated by the infant's, and later the child's projections of his own phantasies. Whatever desires he has himself he attributes to his parents, and in phantasy experiences the parents as exchanging precisely those gratifications that he desires for himself. The parents, objects of so much desire and frustration, become objects of attack in phantasy, but since in the depressive position there is also an awareness of dependence on the parents and love for them, these attacks give rise to feelings of loss, guilt, and depressive anxiety. Against this situation defenses are mobilized. There is a more or less severe regression to the paranoid-schizoid modes of operation. For instance, the parents may be split into an ideal one and a wholly bad one, or the parental couple may be split into ideal nonsexual parents and hateful sexual ones, and so on. Projections may produce such threatening figures as the combined parental figure—often seen by Melanie Klein in the analysis of small children. Manic defenses are put into play involving splitting, on slightly different lines, between destroyed parental figures and idealized and powerful ones with which, in a manic state of mind, the child identifies himself. The working through of the Oedipus complex involves the lessening of those splits and the withdrawal of projections, resulting in the child's growing awareness of his own sexual and aggressive wishes toward his parents. The awareness of aggressive phantasies in relation to loved parental figures brings reparative elements into genital desires and phantasies. Attacks on the internal sexual parents are followed by feelings of guilt and loss, and lead to a wish to restore internally and externally a good sexual couple. This internal restoration of the parental couple provides an internal model for creative and procreative genitality.

All Melanie Klein's earlier work on the Oedipus complex and the superego is encompassed in her later concept of positions, and looking back, from the point of view of the paranoid-schizoid and the depressive position, one can see the early material in a conceptually more orderly manner. For instance, if we look again at the dreams presented by D in relation to the death of his mother, described by Klein in "Mourning and Its Relation to Manic-Depressive States"[1] (see chapter vii above, pages

[1] *Writings* I, pp. 344–69.

83–84), we can tease out of those dreams the paranoid-schizoid and the depressive elements and also, when we compare the first dream with a later one, see a certain movement toward the preponderance of depressive elements. In the first dream,

> *He saw a bull lying in a farmyard. It was not quite dead, and looked very uncanny and dangerous. He was standing on one side of the bull, his mother on the other. He escaped into a house, feeling that he was leaving his mother behind in danger and that he should not do so; but he vaguely hoped that she would get away.*[2] [Klein's italics.]

The various associations, as the reader might remember, led to the conclusion that his father was the dangerous bull, destroying his mother in intercourse. His own aggression is obviously projected into the father. The denial of his mourning is also apparent in his running away and leaving his mother in danger. In the session he omitted to tell the analyst that his mother had died the night before. There are, however, some depressive elements—the bull itself is half-dead and the patient has some concern for his mother, some guilt about leaving her to the danger, and some hope that she would get away. The night after his mother's funeral he had a dream in which a father figure and an analyst figure were trying to help him, but actually he had to fight for his life against them. He said, "Death was claiming me,"[3] and complained bitterly about the analysis disintegrating him. The destroyed internal parents, the dying bull, and the injured mother inside him became persecutors, threatening him with death; his analyst represented them and her offer of help was felt as a threat. On the third night

[2] Ibid., p. 364.
[3] Ibid., p. 366.

after his mother's funeral, he reported the following dream:

> *He saw a bus coming towards him in an uncontrolled way—apparently driving itself. It went towards a shed. He could not see what happened to the shed, but knew definitely that the shed "was going to blazes." Then two people, coming from behind him, were opening the roof of the shed and looking into it. D did not "see the point of their doing this," but they seemed to think it would help.*[4] [Klein's italics.]

Among his associations he referred to the fact that at the beginning of his mother's illness he accidentally ran his car into a post. The blazing shed represented his parents inside him, and in the session he showed much more awareness of his own aggression against the parental couple (he drove the car into the post), and his fear of their destruction in his internal world; this brought him in touch with the mourning for his mother hitherto absent, and with guilt about his own aggression. The projection of his aggression into his father and the splitting and denial represented in the first dream by his running away from the scene in which his mother is in danger were partly defenses against the guilt and mourning in relation to his parents in the depressive position, reawakened by the actual illness and death of his mother.

> While he was going through this mourning with sorrow and despair, his deeply buried love for his mother came more and more into the open, and his relation to both parents altered. On one occasion he spoke of them, in connection with a pleasant childhood memory, as "my dear old parents"—a new departure in him.[5]

The feeling of persecution lessened. In the dream after his mother's funeral he had to fight his analyst and his

[4] Ibid.
[5] Ibid., p. 368.

father. In the dream of the shed the two figures are accepted as helpful.

Looking again at some of the material in *The Psycho-Analysis of Children,* one can see, for instance, Erna's Oedipal material as belonging to a paranoid-schizoid mode of functioning. All the vicious attacks she phantasizes making on her mother's body and her father's penis, seen as part objects, are also projected on to her objects, giving rise to paranoid and hypochondriacal fears. Mrs. Klein drew attention in the description of that case[6] to the importance of the paranoid element in Erna. One can contrast Erna's material with that of Richard. Richard dealt with his Oedipal situation by splitting his mother into an ideal breast mummy and bad genital mother, combined with a bad Hitler father; but throughout his analysis he was struggling with depressive feelings and reparative wishes. For instance: one day when he learned that his analysis was to be interrupted because Mrs. Klein had to go to London he became very aggressive toward her, representing the bad genital mother containing the bad father (the enemies in London); but immediately afterward, having produced a collision between a ship representing himself and one representing his mother and Mrs. Klein:

> Richard put the battleships *Rodney* and *Nelson* (his mother and father) side by side, and then, in a row lengthwise, some ships representing his brother, himself, and his dog, arranged—as he said, in order of age. Here the fleet game was expressing his wish to restore harmony and peace in the family, by allowing his parents to come together and by giving way to his father's and brother's authority.[7]

Mrs. Klein comments thus:

[6] The Psycho-Analysis of Children, *Writings* II.
[7] "The Oedipus Complex in the Light of Early Anxieties" (1945), *Writings* I, p. 378.

. . . Richard was not only dominated by the need to defend himself against the fear of being attacked by his rivals, his father and brother, but also by concern for his good objects. Feelings of love and the urge to repair damage done in phantasy—damage which would be repeated if he gave way to his hatred and jealousy—came out in greater strength.[8]

In Richard, the wish to have intercourse with his mother was reinforced by his reparative wishes to restore her and give her babies.

An identification with the good sexual internal parents, together with love and concern for the external parents, help the child to renounce gradually the sexual possession of the external parents and to transfer his sexual wishes to other objects.

The concept of positions enabled Mrs. Klein also to formulate a comprehensive theory of anxiety and guilt. It is significant that, although the analysis of anxiety had been a guiding principle throughout her work, she only produced one paper dealing specifically with anxiety and guilt.[9] Only after the formulation of the paranoid-schizoid position did she have a conceptual framework which enabled her to formulate more theoretically her views on anxiety and guilt and to relate them in a more consistent manner to Freud. Freud's thinking on anxiety evolved in the course of his work. Originally he considered anxiety to be a direct conversion of the libido, when frustrated. However, he abandoned this view when he discovered that it was anxiety which led to repression, not repression of libidinal wishes to anxiety. He never directly connected anxiety with aggression, but rather with a flood of excitation from whatever source.[10]

[8] Idem.
[9] "On the Theory of Anxiety and Guilt" (1948), *Writings* III, pp. 25–42.
[10] "Inhibitions, Symptoms and Anxiety," *SE* XX.

For Freud, the two basic anxieties are fear of the loss of the object, which may be pre-Oedipal, and castration anxiety, which is the central anxiety of the Oedipus complex. He does not consider the death instinct as a direct source of anxiety, since, according to him, the unconscious and the infant have no concept of death. He views the fear of death as an expression of the fear of castration. Melanie Klein sees anxiety as a direct response to the operation of the death instinct. In her view, the death instinct is deflected in the first place because its operation stirs anxiety, and she sees anxiety as taking two basic forms—persecutory anxiety belonging to the paranoid-schizoid position and depressive anxiety belonging to the depressive position. The fundamental anxiety about the loss of the object postulated by Freud could, according to her, be experienced in either way, or, of course, in any combination of the two: it can be experienced in a paranoid way, as the object turning bad and attacking, or in a depressive way—that is, the object remains good and the anxiety concerns losing the good rather than being attacked by the bad. Castration anxiety is of a predominantly paranoid nature; it centers on the penis, the paranoid anxiety about being attacked by the bad object. Before the primacy of the genital, these anxieties were concerned with being devoured, broken up into pieces, poisoned, and so on. Furthermore, in its more evolved form castration anxiety involves also depressive elements such as the phantasy of losing a good internal penis, felt as a tool of reparation, whose loss therefore arouses the depressive anxiety about one's ability to restore the mother.

Depressive anxiety comes very close to, and is connected with guilt, which makes its appearance in the depressive position. Freud's views on guilt also underwent an evolution. He relates guilt to the operation of the superego and therefore sees it as arising predominantly in connection with the Oedipus complex, although he does make references to guilt in relation to earlier stages, for instance, in relation to cannibalism or to anal sadism. He expresses no disagreement with Ferenczi's formulations about a sphincter morality preceding the superego formation. Originally, Freud considered guilt as being due to the libidinal incestuous impulses. With the hypothesis of the death instinct, his views on guilt changed and he increasingly saw it as related to aggression. His definitive view was that guilt derives solely from destructive impulses. And in "Civilization and Its Discontents" (1930) he relates the severity of the superego to the child's own repressed aggression, acknowledging his agreement with the findings of Melanie Klein and other English writers.[11] For Klein, guilt begins in the depressive position with the recognition of attacks made on an ambivalently loved internal object. The reproaches of that object (remorse) are felt as guilt. As the depressive position evolves and the persecutory elements in the superego diminish, so guilt bcomes less persecutory and gradually becomes a realistic concern for the fate of one's objects, external and internal, and it loses its punitive aspect, which was a continuation of the early paranoid fear.

The shift from the paranoid-schizoid to the depressive position is a fundamental change from psychotic to sane functioning. As the depressive position gains ascendance there is a progressive diminution of omnipotence and of the distortion of perception through projections. External and internal reality become differentiated. The sense of psychic reality develops—acknowledging and assuming responsibility for one's own impulses and the state of one's internal objects. Reality-testing can then take place, and the matching of one's own phantasies with the perception

[11] SE XXI, p. 130, n. 1.

of reality. Concern for the object, a leading characteristic of the depressive position, contributes to reality-testing; there is an anxious scanning of the object to assess its state. The wish to preserve the integrity of the object leads to a gradual abandonment of projective identification and omnipotent control, which leads to an acceptance of reality. Repression gradually takes over from splitting. Unacceptable impulses are dealt with intrapsychically by repression and not in an object-damaging way by projection. There is a fundamental change in object relationships. Splitting and projections, with resulting persecution or idealization, give way to realistic discrimination and a capacity for love and realistic concern within mature object relations which allow for interdependence and acknowledge ambivalence.

This development in turn affects such mental functions as symbol formation and sublimation. In "The Importance of Symbol-Formation in the Development of the Ego" (1930)[12] Klein understood symbol-formation to be linked with projective identification, though at that time she did not use the term. In a later paper[13] she remarks that concern for the object also plays a role in symbol-formation. She did not develop the subject further, but it is possible to see a development in the ability to form and to use symbols as part of the evolution from the paranoid-schizoid to the depressive mode of functioning. In the paranoid-schizoid position, when projective identification is in ascendance, part of the ego becomes identified with the object in a concrete way. Dick, looking at some wood shavings, says, "Poor Mrs. Klein."[14] The symbol and the object are one—the kind of symbol-

[12] *Writings* I.
[13] "Some Theoretical Conclusions Regarding the Emotional Life of the Infant" (1952), *Writings* III, p. 83.
[14] "The Importance of Symbol-Formation in the Development of the Ego" (1930), *Writings* I, p. 227.

formation underlying psychotic concrete thinking. In the depressive position the omnipotent possession of the object is renounced; the object is mourned, and the symbol is needed to replace and to represent the object without being fully identified with it. The symbol becomes non-psychotic and can then be used in sublimation and in communication. Similarly, it is in the depressive position that sublimation and creativity develop. Experiences of guilt and loss in relation to the internal objects give rise to reparative urges to re-create internally and externally the lost internal objects.

Melanie Klein wrote only three papers on art. The first of these, "Infantile Anxiety Situations Reflected in a Work of Art and in the Creative Impulse,"[15] though it was read in 1929, before she had thought of the depressive position, describes beautifully the roots of the creative impulse in the depressive position and the reparative drives associated with it. She discusses Colette's libretto for Ravel's opera, *L'Enfant et les Sortilèges* and an article, "The Empty Space," by Karen Michaelis, about the development of a painter, Ruth Kjar. In Colette's libretto, a little boy whose mother leaves him, threatening "You shall have dry bread and no sugar in your tea!" flies into a rage, attacking furiously inanimate objects around him, as well as a cat and a squirrel. The objects he attacks suddenly grow enormous and retaliate. He flees to the garden, but owls, cats, and squirrels prepare to attack him too. In the scramble a hurt squirrel falls to the ground. Moved to pity, the child picks up the squirrel and binds its paw. Magically the animals become friendly and the world returns to ordinary size. The child whispers "Mamma." Klein analyzes the symbolic meaning of the child's attack on the room, representing his mother's body, and on the various objects representing the father's

[15] *Writings* I, pp. 210–18.

penis and the babies inside her. His attack turns all these objects against him. She does not, in that paper, mention projection, but we would assume that the objects turn bad and frightening not only because the child attacked them but also because of the violence of his projections, leading to a claustrophobic and paranoid situation. At the moment when he picks up the squirrel comes the shift from the paranoid-schizoid position to the depressive position and with it the return of love and reality sense. The monsters which surrounded the child disappear.

Here she describes the shift but does not relate it directly to the creative impulse. This she does in the second example, where she analyzes Karen Michaelis's description of the painter Ruth Kjar. That young woman had a depressive reaction when a picture was removed from the wall in her room. The empty space on the wall "grinned hideously down at her."[16] She was subject to fits of deep depression and clearly the empty space on the wall echoed a desolate aspect of her internal world. She seemed to be in complete despair about the empty space, until suddenly she decided to paint a picture directly on the wall. The picture which she painted was a life-size figure of a naked Negress, and was the beginning of a painting career which lasted a lifetime. Klein, examining the description of her paintings and the sketchy life history, shows how the depression—relating presumably to the destruction of her internal mother, which left a hostile, empty place inside her—was resolved by a symbolic re-creation of her mother in her painting. Klein concludes that the anxieties of the depressive position and the reparative urge which they give rise to lie at the root of creativity.

Depressive anxieties are stirred at every step of development. The realization of the separateness between the

[16] Ibid., p. 215.

baby and the breast, and, later on, weaning, are the source of those attacks on the breast and the mother which are the core of the depressive position. The depressive feelings are reactivated by every loss, and every step in development implies some loss. In toilet training there is the need to renounce an idealized internal stool; achievements in walking and talking also involve acknowledgments of separateness and separation; in adolescence infantile dependence has to be given up; in adulthood one has to face the loss of one's parents and parental figures, and gradually the loss of one's youth. At every step the battle must be waged anew between, on the one hand, regression from the depressive pain to the paranoid-schizoid mode of functioning or, on the other, working through of the depressive pain in a way leading to further growth and development. In that sense one could say that the depressive position is never entirely worked through: the working through of the depressive position would result in something like the perfectly mature individual. But the degree to which the depression has been worked through and internal good objects securely established within the ego determines the maturity and stability of the individual.

Envy and Gratitude

XI

In 1952 Melanie Klein was seventy. She had
started her professional work rather late in life,
when she was nearly forty. By seventy she could
look back on thirty years of creative work. *The
International Journal of Psycho-Analysis* brought
out a birthday issue for her containing eleven
papers by her pupils and colleagues. In 1955
most of those essays plus ten others, including
two by Melanie Klein herself, were produced in
book form under the title *New Directions in
Psycho-Analysis*.[1] This book shows the influence
her work had on many aspects of psychoanalysis. It is divided into two parts: clinical and applied.

The clinical part contains a number of papers
on the analysis of children. One of the papers, by

[1] Edited by M. Klein, P. Heimann, and R. E. Money-
Kyrle.

Emilio Rodrigué,[2] is on the analysis of a three-year-old mute schizophrenic. Rodrigué continues the research begun by Mrs. Klein in her analysis of Dick, and shows the connection between the development of speech and the beginning of the depressive position. There are also two papers on the analysis of adult schizophrenics: Herbert Rosenfield's "Notes on the Psycho-Analysis of the Super-Ego Conflict in an Acute Schizophrenic Patient" (1952), and W. R. Bion's "Language and the Schizophrenic" (1953). These were among the first papers of Rosenfeld and Bion, marking the beginning of their outstanding contributions to the psychoanalysis of psychotics.

Part II contains articles showing the application of Klein's concepts in a variety of fields other than clinical work. It contains her paper "On Identification" (1955), in which she discusses Julien Green's novel *If I Were You*, and describes the phantasy of massive projective identification which, according to her, is its theme. There are two papers on literature by Joan Riviere, and an article by Segal, "A Psychoanalytical Approach to Aesthetics" (1951), in which she applies Klein's concepts of the paranoid-schizoid and depressive positions to the realm of aesthetics. Adrian Stokes's "Form in Art" pursues the same theme, which he went on to develop in many later writings. The article by Money-Kyrle, "Psychoanalysis and Ethics," is similarly the first of many contributions in which he was to examine philosophical problems in the light of Melanie Klein's discoveries. There are also two articles in the field of sociology by W. R. Bion and E. Jaques. Clearly, Melanie Klein's insights have illuminated many fields. Ernest Jones writes in his preface to the book:

[2] "The Analysis of a Three-Year-Old Mute Schizophrenic," *New Directions in Psycho-Analysis,* pp. 140–79.

It is a matter for wide satisfaction as well as for personal congratulation that Mrs Klein has lived to see her work firmly established. So long as it was simply deposited in what she herself had published there was always the hope, but by no means the certainty, that it would be taken up by future students. The situation has now moved beyond that stage; her work is firmly established. As a result of her personal instruction, combined with the insight of those who decided to accept it, she has a considerable number of colleagues and pupils who follow her lead in exploring the deepest depths.[3]

One might have thought that with the completion of her theory of the structure and development of the mind her life's work was achieved. This, however, was not to be. In 1957, first in a paper on envy, and then in the short book, *Envy and Gratitude*,[4] she put forward another hypothesis that was to shake the psychoanalytical world and give rise to fresh controversies.

The concept of envy had of course been used in psychoanalytical practice and theory before Melanie Klein, but, as is the case in common speech, envy was not clearly distinguished from related notions such as jealousy or rivalry. Though Freud and others referred to the boy's envy of femininity and child-bearing as an aspect of his negative Oedipus complex, envy was given a prominent place as a powerful feeling distinct from jealousy only in the case of the little girl's envy of the penis. This was considered of such fundamental importance that Freud, for instance, thought it to be the basis of negative therapeutic reaction and interminable analysis in women. Melanie Klein, even in her early work, attached considerable importance to the analysis of envy in all its aspects. She considered penis envy in girls a much more

[3] Preface to *New Directions in Psycho-Analysis* (1955). Reprinted as Appendix to *Writings* III, p. 341.
[4] *Writings* III, p. 176–235.

complex phenomenon than Freud thought, and not of a primary nature. In her paper "The Oedipus Complex in the Light of Early Anxieties" (1945) she states that she considers penis envy to be an expression of the girl's bisexuality, and to exist in its own right, as described by Freud, but she holds that it is reinforced from two sources. One is the girl's envy of her mother's body, which, in the early stages of the Oedipus complex, is felt to contain father's penis and babies. Thus her first envy in relation to the penis is related to her envy of the mother. The second source of envy lies in the frustrated desire for the possession of her father's penis in sexual intercourse. In the development of the boy, Klein emphasizes his envy of mother's body as containing the penis and the babies, considering this an important element in the negative Oedipus complex.

In her new writing, however, she singles out envy as one of the fundamental and most primitive emotions. For the first time she formulates her view that envy arises in earliest infancy and in its fundamental primitive form is directed at the feeding breast. The love, care, and food received from the mother stir in the infant two opposite reactions: one of gratification leading to love, a primitive form of gratitude; the other of hostility and envy, based on the realization that the source of food, love, and comfort lies outside one's self. Those feelings are not related to the experience of the physical feeding only. For the gratified infant, the breast becomes the source of mental as well as physical qualities; he idealizes the breast and experiences it as the fount of love, understanding, wisdom, and creativity, since it is capable of converting his state of distress into one of contentment and happiness. Envy of the breast is stirred by gratification, because gratification is proof of the infinite richness of the breast's resources. But envy can also, paradoxically, be stirred by frustration and deprivation. Since the infant idealizes the breast in his phantasy, when he is deprived he assumes that the riches he attributes to the breast are enjoyed by the breast itself.

A patient of Mrs. Klein's had to miss two sessions, and was afraid that she might miss a third one. Returning to her analysis full of grievances, she reported the following dream:

> She was in a restaurant, seated at a table; however nobody came to serve her. She decided to join a queue and fetch herself something to eat. In front of her was a woman who took two or three little cakes and went away with them. The patient also took two or three little cakes.[5]

The patient hesitated about the name of the cakes and at first called them *"petit fru"* which reminded her of *"petite Frau"*—Frau Klein.

> The analyst who went away with the two or three *petits fours* stood not only for the breast which was withheld, but also for the breast which was going to *feed itself*. . . .
>
> To frustration had thus been added envy of the breast. This envy had given rise to bitter resentment, for the mother had been felt to be selfish and mean, feeding and loving herself rather than her baby.

Jealousy as well as envy added to the frustration:

> In the analytic siuation I was suspected of having enjoyed myself during the time when she was absent, or of having given the time to other patients whom I preferred. The queue which the patient had decided to join referred to other more favoured rivals.

Klein draws careful distinctions between the related concepts of jealousy, envy, and greed. Envy is more primitive than jealousy; it arises in a part-object relation and

[5] Ibid., p. 205.

is not related to a triangular situation. It is purely destructive and aimed at the object of love and admiration. Jealousy is a more sophisticated feeling belonging to the Oedipal triangle. It is based on love, and the hatred of the rival is a function of the love for the object of desire. Klein quotes Crabb's *English Synonyms*, which states that jealousy can be noble or ignoble, but envy is always ignoble. Greed also has to be differentiated from envy. Greed aims at possession of all the richness of the object, beyond the need of the self or the capacities or willingness of the object. The damage done in greed is incidental. In envy the direct aim is to spoil the attributes of the object. This spoiling also has a defensive aspect, since, if the enviable characteristics are destroyed, one no longer has the painful experience of the feeling of envy. Thus, spoiling is both an expression of and a defense against envy. Greed operates mainly by introjection; envy by destructive projective identification.

These three kinds of feeling are of course related and they interact. The intractable element and spoiling aspect of greed may cover up envy: one can be greedy in order to spoil. Greed may also be used as a defense against envy; this is based on a phantasy that if one could possess oneself of everything, there would be no need for envy to arise. Excessive pathological jealousy may also conceal envy. When the primitive envy is not excessive, the Oedipal envy of the rival's attributes springs out of jealousy in relation to the loved object; for instance, the father's penis is envied because that is what makes him mother's preferred sexual partner. When envy is strong, the reverse is true. The rival's attributes are envied and the possession of the object is sought not primarily out of desire for the object, but out of an overriding envy of the rival. The existence of strong envy, as a component of jealousy, influences deeply the fate of the Oedipus complex. In the little girl, when the envy of the mother is strong, the father is desired rather as an additional attribute of the mother's than as a loved object in his own right. This may set up a pattern in adult life in which a man is desired only if he is felt to be attached to another woman. In the little boy, excessive envy of the mother may lead to a predominantly negative Oedipus complex and in later life to a bad relation with women or to homosexuality. Penis envy is also deeply influenced by the more primitive envy of the breast. The infant may turn away in hatred from the envied breast to an idealized penis, which in turn becomes a carrier of the original envy of the breast. Thus, Klein's earlier view of penis envy as autonomous, although reinforced from other sources (1945),[6] is supplanted by the more radical hypothesis that the primary origin of excessive penis envy must be sought in the infant's envy of the breast.

Since it operates from earliest infancy, envy, if excessive, becomes a fundamental element in the pathology of both the paranoid-schizoid and the depressive positions. Following her formulation of the depressive position, Klein always emphasized the introjection of the breast as a good and trustworthy object—the core both of the ego and of a helpful superego. Envy, since it attacks the goodness of the object, interferes, of course, in such an introjection. In the paranoid-schizoid position splitting between a good and a bad object is a necessary pre-condition of the introjection of a good breast. Envy attacks the good object and, by projection and fragmentation, makes it bad; therefore it produces a state of confusion between good and bad, which is at the root of many psychotic confusions. Envious attacks on the ideal breast preclude the introjection of a good object which

[6] "The Oedipus Complex in the Light of Early Anxieties," *Writings* I.

would strengthen the ego. This gives rise to a painful vicious circle. The more the good internal object is destroyed, the more impoverished the ego feels, and this in turn increases envy. The projection of envy into the object gives rise to an envious superego. The oversevere superego, which Freud describes as the basis of psychical disturbance, often turns out on analysis to be an envious superego. That is, its attacks are directed not only against the individual's aggression but also, and even predominantly, against the individual's progressive and creative capacities.

The operation of envy in the paranoid-schizoid position, through projections into the object, increases and maintains persecutory anxieties, and, through the lack of good internal figures, makes these anxieties harder to overcome. In the depressive position, envy maintains a persecutory aspect of guilt, increases it, and adds hopelessness to it. Anger, due to frustration, may be overcome when gratification returns. Jealousy can be relieved by love from the loved object and is mitigated by ambivalence toward the rival who, in the Oedipal situation, is also an object of love. For envy, however, there is little relief. An envious attack on a loved object, stimulated by its very goodness, gives rise to intense guilt and feelings of hopelessness. Envy also interferes with reparation. A full restoration of the object to its original state of intactness and integrity is incompatible with envy. Only a manic reparation can be attempted in which the object is partially repaired, but the self remains in a superior position.

Because of the pain and the anxiety it causes, excessive envy also mobilizes powerful defenses which interfere with the gradual evolution from the paranoid-schizoid to the depressive position. If envy is strong in the paranoid-schizoid position, projection is increased, the object is devalued, and envy is projected into the devalued object.

Thus, the paranoid anxieties are increased. To defend against that, in turn, splitting may be reinforced and excessive idealization used to counteract the persecution. This excessive idealization prevents a gradual integration of an ideal object. At the same time, being based on a denial of persecution, it is both rigid and unstable. Since excessive idealization increases the envy, thus establishing a vicious circle, the idealized object can quickly turn into an object of hatred and persecution. This may lead to a premature turning from the breast to the alternative object, the penis, and therefore to premature sexualization. Klein had noticed this premature sexualization in the analysis of Dick,[7] the psychotic child, but hadn't at the time seen it as a defense against envy. Other schizoid mechanisms, such as the stifling of all feelings, in particular the stifling of love and admiration to avoid the mobilization of envy, are reinforced.

In the depressive position, the integration of the good and bad objects becomes much more difficult, because the recognition of envious attacks on and the devaluation of the good object give rise to a persecutory guilt and a feeling of hopelessness. Reparation, as we have said above, is impeded and manic mechanisms of defense are reinforced.

In the analytic setting, the combination of envy and defenses against it lead to negative therapeutic reactions. These can vary from day-to-day fluctuations between progress and regression to severe massive reactions. For instance, Mrs. Klein quotes the case of a patient who during the analytic session had arrived at a satisfactory solution of an external problem. In the next session he was full of complaints that the previous one had aroused his anxiety. He was annoyed to realize that he needed the

[7] "The Importance of Symbol-Formation in the Development of the Ego," *Writings* I.

session to find the solution to his problem. The fact that he needed the analyst's help, and got it, aroused in him envy and the wish to devalue and reject the analyst. This kind of reaction had to be analyzed in him over and over again. She describes a more extreme reaction in a woman with severe manic-depressive psychopathology. This woman, during her analysis, had achieved an important professional success. This produced a feeling of great elation and triumph. She had the following dream:

> In the dream she was up in the air on a magic carpet which supported her and was above the top of a tree. She was sufficiently high up to look through a window into a room where a cow was munching something which appeared to be an endless strip of blanket. In the same night she also had a bit of a dream in which her pants were wet.[8]

The cow in previous dreams had regularly represented the analyst as the breast-feeding mother.

> She associated that the endless strip of blanket represented an endless stream of words, and it occurred to her that these were all the words I had ever said in the analysis and which I now had to swallow.[9]

Cowed by the patient's success, the analyst was to eat her words. The wet pants represented urinary attacks on the analyst. The analytic help that this patient received had mobilized powerful envy, leading to the devaluation and destruction of the analyst, representing the original breast. This destruction of her good internal object and the persecution and guilt arising out of it led to a deep depression. Progress in this patient led to a negative therapeutic reaction which was recurrent and severe.

When envy is very strong, it may be split off, and even if serious pathology does not develop, the personality be-

[8] *Writings* III, p. 207.
[9] Ibid., pp. 207–208.

comes impoverished and the whole relationship to a good internal object is felt to be insecure. In analysis, steps toward integration of that split-off envy arouse enormous anxiety. Even in the relatively normal individual, the split-off envious part of the personality is linked with psychotic anxieties and mechanisms, and their appearance arouses a fear of madness. For instance, Klein quotes a patient who had gradually become more aware of envy, both toward an older sister and her mother. She reported a dream in which

> she was alone in a railway carriage with a woman, of whom she could only see the back, who was leaning towards the door of the compartment in great danger of falling out. The patient held her strongly, grasping her by the belt with one hand; with the other hand she wrote a notice to the effect that a doctor was engaged with a patient in this compartment and should not be disturbed, and she put up this notice on the window.[10]

Her associations revealed that the figure on whom she kept a tight grasp represented a mad part of herself. Madness was associated to her envy of her sister and her mother's breasts. Her holding on to the figure represented her wish to integrate that part of herself and, indeed, in her case, the integration of those envious feelings led to a revaluation of her sister and the recovery of her love for her. Some of her madness had been projected into her sister, whom she used to consider very neurotic. The understanding of her feelings led both to the revaluation of her sister and to a gradual healing of a split in herself. But her initial reaction to these discoveries was shock and a fear of madness.

Envy normally plays a part in every infant's dependent relation to the breast. In favorable development, it is over-

[10] Ibid., p. 209.

come by feelings of love and gratification in which the good experience gives rise to gratitude. When envy is counteracted by love and gratitude, it becomes manageable, and the need to split it off or project it is not so strong. In the depressive position it is further modified by love, and becomes a normal component of the Oedipal jealousy, gradually muted into integrated feelings of rivalry and emulation. In the psychoanalytical situation if split-off envy can be analyzed and integrated, there is a great freeing and enrichment of the psychoanalytical relationship and of the patient's whole personality.

What accounts for the excessive strength of envy in certain infants? Certainly external circumstances, as in all development, play an extremely important role. Klein suggested how frustration may, paradoxically, lead to envy. Other external factors, which she does not go into, but which were worked out by her collaborators, can also play a part. For instance: an excessively narcissistic mother, unable to cope with the infant's projections and keeping herself as an idealized object, puts the infant in a constantly devalued position in relation to herself, which increases his envy. But Klein emphasized strongly that there is also an internal, constitutional factor, which varies from infant to infant. She follows Abraham, who spoke of a constitutionally strong oral component, but in her view this constitutional component is oral envy.

The discoveries she made late in her career, and her conviction that excessive envy may be constitutionally determined, modified somewhat her therapeutic optimism. She believed that analysis and integration of the split-off envy could lead to the overcoming of the negative therapeutic reaction, and therefore make analysis more effective. At the same time, however, she thought that in certain cases envy was rooted in unalterable constitutional factors and so powerful that no integration could be achieved.

Her book, and the paper which had preceded it, initiated a storm of controversy. It was contended that an infant would not be capable of such a sophisticated feeling as envy, and while rage and frustration were conceivable, envy, aroused by a good experience, was not. It was also contended that Klein was reverting to the doctrine of the original sin, which she recast as envy, and generally that she "blames too much on the infant." In some ways this was a continuation of the controversy over how much ego and object awareness there is at birth. It also revived the conflict between the view that inherent aggressiveness plays a significant role in the child's history, and the view which holds aggression to be purely reactive. Klein's hypothesis about envy is compatible with her other views about the primitive ego and its capacity for object relationships. There are links between her theory of primitive envy and Freud's of primary narcissism. Freud says that hatred toward one's objects is older than love. On realizing that the source of life is outside himself, the child reacts with narcissistic rage. This narcissistic rage can be seen as destructive envy. But Freud sees narcissism as primary and long-lasting, and narcissistic rage as appearing only in the second anal phase. In Klein's view, object relationships coexist with narcissism from the beginning, and envy is experienced in the first oral phase. Narcissism can be reinforced as a defense against envy, and excessive narcissism is in fact defensive rather than primary. Nor does Klein think that hate is older than love; and though she was criticized for attributing too much importance to aggression, unlike Freud, she sees love as also existing from the beginning and as playing an essential role in psychological growth and integration.

The Last Years

Envy and Gratitude (1957) was Melanie Klein's last major contribution to theory. She wrote comparatively few papers in the remaining four years of her life. Feeling that her theoretical work was complete, in 1958 she wrote a metapsychological paper, "On the Development of Mental Functioning."[1] Here she returns to Freud's theory of the conflict between the life and death instinct, and stresses again that she treats it not as a biological speculation but as the actual instinctual basis of love and hate. She elaborates her view of the mental structure in terms of the object relationships and the life and death instinct. There is one new and surprising feature in this paper. Whereas in her earlier writings she emphasized that the archaic objects, the ideal and persecutory part objects, are the roots of the superego and become integrated in the depressive position, she now

1 *Writings* III, pp. 236–46.

argues that the superego from the beginning has some integration, and that those archaic objects remain split off into what she describes as "the deepest unconscious." The problem of whether one does or does not call those figures "superego" is a matter of more than merely terminological importance. The emphasis in the earlier papers seems to be on the point that the greater the integration achieved, and the lesser the degree of splitting off in relation to the unavoidably remaining part-object relations, the better the prospects for the individual's mental health. Here, on the contrary, she holds that those archaic objects should remain split off and that it is the failure of such splitting, a sudden irruption of split-off archaic objects, that brings about a psychotic breakdown. She does not compare or contrast this view with the earlier one, and it remains unclear whether she was aware that she had in fact changed her mind on this matter. It seems more likely that she had not elaborated the point sufficiently and remained unaware of the apparent contradiction. Possibly what she had in mind is that the ideal state of integration is never achieved, that the archaic persecutory objects remain split off, and that the point at issue is the relative strength of the integrated part and the remaining paranoid-schizoid objects. If the unintegrated part which is split off is too strong it may invade and destroy the integrated part of the ego.

This paper does not do justice to her best work, maybe because it is purely metapsychological, which is not her natural style. The strength of her work and her formulations lies in their closeness to the actual clinical material and even her theory of the paranoid-schizoid position and the depressive position can be seen as based on clinical concepts and as adhering very closely to clinical experience.

Apart from this paper, she wrote one of her rare essays for nonpsychoanalysts, on "Our Adult World and Its

Roots in Infancy" (1959),[2] based on a talk given to a group of sociologists. There she conveys how the child's earliest relationships—those which form his internal world—are the basis of his view of the world as a whole. This in turn determines social as well as personal relationships in adulthood. She had started a paper on *The Oresteia*,[3] which she had not finished at the time of her death. The last Congress she attended was the 21st Congress in Copenhagen in 1959. She made there a short contribution to a discussion of depression in the schizophrenic, and presented a paper, "On the Sense of Loneliness,"[4] but she was not satisfied with it, and was still working on it at the time of her death. The paper was obviously related to her own growing sense of loneliness.

While Klein was working on the paper on envy she went through a phase of some depression and growing pessimism. She felt very unsure of the acceptance and survival of her own work, pessimistic about the future of psychoanalysis and more generally about the survival of values in the world. (It was also a time when people were sharply conscious of the threat of nuclear war.) Her psychological evolution at this point bore great similarities to Freud's. He had become very pessimistic following his work on the death instinct, a pessimism he expresses in *Civilization and Its Discontents*. Similarly Melanie Klein's work on envy, which she considered an expression of the death instinct, led to an increasing pessimism. Other factors probably contributed. She was very grieved by the death of Lola Brook, her secretary and a friend of many years' standing. Her friendship with one of her major collaborators and supporters, Paula Heimann, came to an end between the time of the

[2] Ibid., pp. 247–63.
[3] "Some Reflections on *The Oresteia*" (1963), ibid., pp. 275–99.
[4] Ibid., pp. 300–13.

publication of the "Notes on Some Schizoid Mechanisms" and that of *Envy and Gratitude*. Major differences had developed between Heimann and Klein, leading not only to disagreements but to personal resentment and bitterness on both sides. And, as with Freud, the threat of her own approaching death may have contributed to her fear about the survival of her work. This phase of pessimism, however, did not last. In some uncompleted autobiographical notes which she left she says that gradually her confidence in the future returned; she was encouraged to see that many of her pupils and followers were engaged in creative work, based on her own and developing it further. She was gratified by the personal support of a number of friends and colleagues. She was also very happy in her growing-up family of grandchildren, and felt particularly close to Michael, the eldest. Though Mrs. Klein retained a close relationship with her son and her daughter-in-law, neither of them deeply shared her interests. Michael, on the other hand, who was approaching adulthood, was a promising scientist, with a lively interest in intellectual pursuits and in Mrs. Klein's work. As he expressed it later, she had become for him more than just the good granny of his childhood. He had reached an age at which he could appreciate her greatness and feel privileged in having a close relationship with her.

Nevertheless, her sense of loneliness must have been growing, and she never completed her paper on that theme. In it she describes various pathological roots of loneliness; in the depressive feeling of the loss of the object, and in the schizoid splits which lead to the deepest loneliness of being cut off from one's own self. These are inevitable, even in the healthy personality, and she returned again and again to the essential loneliness of the human condition.

In the last few years she had gradually reduced her

clinical work, and by 1960 she had only three patients in analysis, but she kept up all her other activities—supervisions, teaching at the Institute, private seminars. She continued to attend regularly scientific meetings in the British Society and took an active part in the discussions. Her main preoccupation, however, was writing the *Narrative of a Child Psycho-Analysis*. She thought that she probably would not make any more major original contributions, and she felt that there was one task she had left unfinished. She had always planned to publish a detailed account of day-by-day sessions with a patient, to leave a picture of her actual work that would be as full, precise, and faithful as could be achieved. An extract of clinical material, even a fairly long one, and clinical illustrations here and there, do not give a sufficient idea of an analyst's work. Many of the criticisms of her work were, she felt, based on misunderstandings and ignorance of her actual work—which was perhaps unavoidable, as it is so difficult to convey in writing the evolution of a psychoanalytic relationship. She wanted to give an account complete enough to warrant well-based critical examination.

While in Pitlochry during the war she carried out an analysis of a ten-year-old boy, Richard, the length of which was limited to four months, the time Richard's family spent there. She had kept detailed notes of Richard's sessions with a view to publishing them at some future date, but never had enough leisure to carry out this project. In the last years of her life, taking fewer patients and feeling relieved of the daily pressure of psychoanalytical work and free also of the pressure of new ideas, the elaboration and publication of which had always taken priority over editing the notes on Richard, she could now devote herself almost fully to this task. The analysis of Richard was particularly suitable for her intentions. As it was a very short analysis, ninety-three sessions in all, she could publish it in its entirety without making the size of the book unmanageable. Also Richard was a lively, imaginative, cooperative child and his material lent itself very well to illustrating both the child's phantasy life and Mrs. Klein's technique. In some ways this analysis was not typical because both analyst and patient knew that the time was limited and relatively short. Also the setting was far from rigorous; Mrs. Klein had no proper playroom of her own and had to share a room that at other times was used by Girl Guides. Pitlochry is a small town; the boy had some access to information about Mrs. Klein, and there were more accidental meetings between them than would have been desirable. Despite these shortcomings, however, Mrs. Klein thought that this analysis basically adhered to her principles of psychoanalytic technique and therefore could be used to show her work in detail.

Richard's parents brought him to treatment mostly because of the child's increasing anxiety and depression. This became manifest at the age of eight when he started school. He was frightened of other children, did not want to go to school, and gradually became afraid even of going out by himself. He was also excessively worried and concerned about his parents, frequently hypochondriacal and depressed. He got on best with women, in relation to whom he tended to be a little seductive and ingratiating. As the analysis progressed, what emerged most clearly were his struggles with the depressive position. Richard, who had a short and unsatisfactory breast-feeding, had a very ambivalent relation to the breast and to his mother. The attacks he made in phantasy on his mother and her breast led to a profound depression which he could not deal with. The hostility to his mother was augmented by Oedipal jealousy in relation to his father, by jealousy of his older brother, and even more by jealousy of phantasied unborn children. He dealt with this painful situation by splitting. He idealized a breast mother and turned all his hostility on to his father and the father's penis. The genital mother associated with father became likewise a terrifying and bad object. His fear of other children and men was linked with his phantasy that he had attacked the babies and the father's penis inside his mother's body. This way of dealing with his ambivalence to his mother influenced deeply the evolution of his Oedipus complex. In his unconscious his father was the butt of the split-off hatred Richard felt toward the breast, and therefore in his phantasy he became such a bad and hated figure that Richard could not cope with his Oedipal rivalry with him.

In his analysis Mrs. Klein could elaborate the relation between the depressive position and the Oedipus complex, showing both how the addition of the Oedipal jealousy increases the infant's ambivalence toward the breast and conversely, how the relation to the breast influences decisively the course of the Oedipus complex. Much of the material that Mrs. Klein gives in her paper "The Oedipus Complex in the Light of Early Anxieties,"[5] comes from the analysis of Richard; and in the *Narrative* one can see in detail the clinical foundations of the theory.

The *Narrative of a Child Psycho-Analysis* makes fascinating reading. One can follow gradually the unfolding of the child's internal world, his phantasies, anxieties, and defenses, and the gradual changes that occur, particularly the decrease in splitting, so that instead of the picture of an ideal breast mummy and a horrible genital mother fused and confused with a bad father, often represented by Hitler, he gradually comes to see his parents

[5] *Writings* I, pp. 370–419.

more as whole people in a relationship which makes him jealous but which does not destroy his love for them. In particular, his relation to his father altered, and repressed love and admiration for him could be mobilized.

This account also provides a much better picture of Klein's technique than is given, for instance, in *The Psycho-Analysis of Children*. One is struck by its fine sense of proportion and balance. There is an easy movement from the interpreting of the transference to interpreting the child's relation to his real parents, and an equilibrium is sustained between the internal and the external. Contrary to the often-held opinion that Mrs. Klein interpreted only phantasy and did not take into account external reality, one can observe in Richard's sessions the impact of many external events that kept impinging on him, such as the absences and returns of his father, visits from his older brother, his mother's indispositions, and many other incidents, with the news of the war, sometimes good sometimes bad, always in the background, increasing Richard's anxiety or, on the contrary, giving him hope. These external events Melanie Klein always connects with the child's own phantasies, showing him how his phantasies color and give an interpretation to those events, and how external happenings in turn increase or decrease his anxieties. She sustains as well a balance between interpreting the past and the present, showing Richard how past experiences like weaning influenced the kind of internal object relationships he had developed and was repeating both in the transference and in his relationships outside.

Apart from carefully editing her notes on the material, Klein added postscript notes to almost all sessions. In those notes she looks at her work of 1940 and appraises it from her new point of view. In many places she criticizes her own technique, sometimes for not being rigorous enough; in others she shows how at the present date she would have gone further in her interpretations. For instance, she points to examples of projective identification which she had not picked up sufficiently. Most important, perhaps, she throws a retrospective light on the dynamic force, shown in many sessions, of Richard's envy, which she had interpreted only occasionally and never consistently followed through. Looking back one could see that Richard was very preoccupied with Mrs. Klein's analytical skill and very ambivalent about it. There are recurring conjunctions in which a feeling of admiration for the analyst's skill is immediately followed by play symbolizing attacks on the breast in a context of fragmentation and splitting, which she described later as characteristic of the paranoid-schizoid position. Richard's envy of the breast is particularly related to its creativity. It is interpretations which he finds new, illuminating and exciting that seem to provoke the attack, and often in those situations he depicts the breast as full of babies. Typical in this respect are, for instance, sessions 66[6] and 67.[7]

In session 66, Richard showed a strong positive transference and appreciation of the analytical work. He was surprised when Mrs. Klein interpreted something which corresponded exactly to a feeling he had expressed to his mother the previous day. Later in the session, he said that this work helped him. Toward the end of the session, looking at Mrs. Klein, he said he was very fond of her. But side by side with those expressions of love and admiration there were split-off attacks. For instance, when Mrs. Klein, in relation to a drawing, interpreted to him his desire for the breast, and the two genitals, his own and his father's, competing for the breast, Richard looked

[6] *Writings* IV, p. 326.
[7] Ibid., p. 332.

at Mrs. Klein, said he was very fond of her, but soon added that he had called the cook an "impudent old fish cadger."[8] Later on, after putting his arm round Mrs. Klein and saying that he loved her, he looked out of the window where there was a hen in the garden, shouting, "Silly old hen,"[9] and when an old woman was passing, "Nasty old woman."[10] So that expressions of love and admiration were immediately followed by angry attacks on the cook—the person who gave him food, standing for the breast—in an attempt to deflect his hostility from Mrs. Klein. She interpreted those attacks in terms of frustration and did not in this session relate them to envy which, she later understood, was stimulated whenever he felt full of love and admiration.

In the next session he arrived two minutes late, and asked Mrs. Klein to keep him two minutes longer. When she interpreted the two minutes as the two breasts which he was afraid of losing, he livened up and said, "You are very clever to find this out. . . ."[11] But soon after he made a drawing of an ice rink, with many dots representing people, and commented that the people were scratching the ice. He also associated this drawing to another one which he had made previously and called a "Chinese protest."[12] The "Chinese protest" at that time had represented urinary and fecal attacks. Mrs. Klein interpreted his drawing and his thought that it might be another "Chinese protest" as an attack on the breast-ice rink, and she related this attack to deprivation, and connected it with weaning.

Soon his material showed him extending the attack to his mother's babies. Mrs. Klein connected all those ac-

[8] Ibid., p. 329.
[9] Ibid., p. 331.
[10] Ibid.
[11] Ibid., p. 332.
[12] Ibid., p. 333.

tivities to his anger with the breast because of deprivation and jealousy of the new babies. A little later in the
session Richard made a drawing of a station, which he
called "Blueing." He said that blue meant light blue, and
he pointed at Mrs. Klein. She asked him whether he could
say anything about "-ing"; he said he did not know, and
Mrs. Klein suggested that it could stand for ink. Richard
smiled and said he knew it, but did not want to say so.
Light blue regularly represented for Richard his ideal
breast mummy. Ink, which he called smelly, represented
his urine and feces. So Mrs. Klein interpreted to him his
wish to split and to keep the light blue mother protected
from his urinary and fecal attacks. Listening to the interpretation, Richard drew an oval outline containing two big
circles and a small one, then he drew two rough circles
outside the oval shape and began to cover them furiously
with dots. After that he made more and more dots in the
oval, grinding his teeth, flashing his eyes, and expressing
rage with his whole face. Mrs. Klein interpreted that the
two circles represented the breasts, hers and his mummy's, and that Richard was attacking them by biting
and grinding with his teeth, and also with the penis,
represented by the pencil, stabbing and urinating. When
she asked him what the shapes inside the oval were, he
replied without hesitation that they were eggs. Mrs. Klein
interpreted the attack on his mother's body and the babies
she contained and related it to the jealousy of the new
babies. In this sequence again one can see how admiration for Mrs. Klein's interpretations, her knowing what
two minutes meant, her guessing that "-ing" represented
ink, led to a phantasy of a breast full of babies, and an
attack which results in a splitting and in the fragmentation of that breast. In her notes on the session, Klein
comments that while deprivation and jealousy certainly
played a role, she now would have interpreted the regular

recurrence of envious attacks following expressions of relief or admiration.

This kind of material and its elaboration in the comments that Klein added later show the experiences which led her to formulate the concept of primitive envy.

Melanie Klein devoted a great deal of time and care to the *Narrative of a Child Psycho-Analysis*. She felt fortunate in having been able to complete it before dying, and when she went to the hospital for her final illness she was sent the proofs of the index and, at the times when she was well enough to do it, she spent her time revising it.

The *Narrative* is a considerable achievement. Not only does it give, as Klein intended, a complete picture of her technique in the analysis of a latency child but, more than that, it shows the development of her thought and illustrates how her theoretical ideas were derived from actual clinical experience.

Toward the end of the summer term of 1960 she had begun to feel very exhausted and unwell. The cause of this malaise was misdiagnosed. Understandably, perhaps, the doctor in charge of her thought that her fatigue was a natural consequence of her working hard and being so active for a person of her advanced years. She went on a summer holiday accompanied and looked after by her grandson Michael, who became very alarmed at her state. She stayed a few weeks in Switzerland with her pupil and friend, Mrs. Esther Bick, getting progressively weaker. Finally, she had a severe hemorrhage. Back in London an operable cancer was diagnosed and she was taken to University College Hospital.

Once in the hospital she felt very relieved, and hoped for a recovery; she felt she was still enjoying life, had many projects for the future and did not welcome the idea of dying; but she was also apprehensive, and made all her preparations for death. She left to colleagues close to her careful instructions about her supervisees and her remaining patients, and she discussed the policy for future publications, giving the full copyright to the Melanie Klein Trust (set up in 1955 with the aim of furthering psychoanalytical research and teaching). She made sure that the proofs of the *Narrative of a Child Psycho-Analysis* were revised and corrected with particular care. She discussed her funeral arrangements, stressing again that it was particularly important to her that no religious service of any description should be part of them. She wanted to leave no false impressions.

The operation was successful and there were no secondaries. Her doctors in the hospital, family, friends, and she herself felt very optimistic. Nevertheless, a few days after the operation she had a secondary hemorrhage and died a few hours later.

Despite her age and the gravity of her illness, this death produced surprise and shock. She had been so active and creative up to the last moment, so present and well in touch with her friends, her family and the psychoanalytical community, that her death was felt as unexpected and untimely.

Melanie Klein: The Person and Her Work

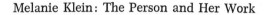

It is probably too soon to assess the full impact of Melanie Klein's work on the development of psychoanalytical theory and practice. The impetus that her ideas gave to research is still active and much new work based on them is still in progress. There is little doubt that her work had not only a profound influence on technique but that it contributed to a change in the psychoanalytical approach to the understanding of the mind—in the psychoanalytical *Weltanschauung*. Freud's work lends itself to many developments. One trend in his theory is linked with his desire to see psychoanalysis wedded firmly to a biological basis. What he called the economic viewpoint, that is, his first instinct theory—the theory of cathexis, countercathexis, instinctual discharge, regression due to blocking of the discharge, and so on—is based on the physicist's model of energy transformation.

On the other hand, his theory of the Oedipus complex and much of his actual clinical work is based on the observation and analysis of object relations. The two, of course, are not contradictory, but it is the relative emphasis given to these factors which determines the psychological outlook.

Melanie Klein, though starting from Freud's final theory of instincts, sees them as manifesting themselves in the interplay of love and hatred in relation to objects, and her work shifts the focus from economic, physical considerations to the importance of object relationships as fundamental determinants of personality:

> The hypothesis that a stage extending over several months precedes object-relations implies that—except for the libido attached to the infant's own body—impulses, phantasies, anxieties, and defences either are not present in him, or are not related to an object, that is to say, they would operate *in vacuo*. The analysis of very young children has taught me that there is no instinctual urge, no anxiety situation, no mental process which does not involve objects, external or internal; in other words, object-relations are at the *centre* of emotional life. Furthermore, love and hatred, phantasies, anxieties, and defences are also operative from the beginning and are *ab initio* indivisibly linked with object-relations. This insight showed me many phenomena in a new light.[1] [Mrs. Klein's italics.]

This change of focus is related to two other interlinked factors. One is the importance of the first two years of life, the other the role of phantasy. In Freud's theory, the nodal point of development is the Oedipus complex at the age of three or four. Manifestations of pre-genital characteristics are seen mainly as regressions from the Oedipus complex. This is linked with the fact that, by and large, Freud and, at times, Abraham, considered that object relationships developed only in the phallic

1 *Writings* III, pp. 52–53.

phase. True, Freud says that the instinct's first object is the breast, but he claims that the infant soon turns to his own body in auto-erotism. And he describes the pregenital stages of development primarily in terms of auto-erotism and narcissism. For him the satisfaction of instinct is independent of object-seeking. But Melanie Klein considered object-seeking to be fundamental, and saw auto-erotism and narcissism as the outcome of the vicissitudes of object relationships. Freud discovered the existence of an internal world, but his description of it centers on one internal object, the superego. Klein widened this understanding by the detailed study of internal phantasy life with complex internal object relationships evolving from earliest infancy.

Freud presents his theories in three conceptual frameworks: descriptive, dynamic, and structural. The descriptive, known as the *topographic* model of the mind, describes the layers of the mind: conscious, pre-conscious, and unconscious. The dynamic, or *economic,* model describes the vicissitudes of instincts and psychic energy. The *structural* model describes the interaction between the ego, superego, and the id. The theory of the paranoid-schizoid and the depressive positions extended Freud's structural theory of the mind. Both the ego and the superego are further analyzed in structural terms. This enlarged structural theory has given a more precise diagnostic tool. It provides for a differentiation between psychotic and neurotic processes, with a place for borderline phenomena at the interface of the two positions, and allows a comprehensive view of neurosis and character formation in terms of the evolution from the paranoid-schizoid to the depressive modes of functioning. This gives a yardstick for measuring the progress of an analysis, and a framework in which to assess fluctuations, even in individual sessions.

The influence Melanie Klein had on psychoanalytic

technique begins with child analysis, and extends beyond the work of her immediate followers and pupils. The play technique she evolved is the basis of psychoanalytic play therapy, now almost universally accepted and widely used throughout the world. In the psychoanalysis of adults, the shift in focus from instincts seeking discharge to object relationships emphasized the role of the transference, and Klein's technique gives more weight to the transference than does the classical Freudian technique. The evolution of the transference in the psychoanalytic process, rather than the reconstruction of the past, became the center of attention. This continues a development which Freud himself initiated. Freud at first thought that "hysterics suffer mainly from reminiscences,"[2] and he saw transference as the reliving of a memory. Thus he could assume that to reconvert transference into memory would be enough to solve the patient's problem. Later, however, he came to think that the patient suffered not only from repressed memories but from repressed impulses, and that it was those impulses which were remobilized by the transference, so giving the patient another chance of working them through. The working through in the transference then became more important than the actual reconstruction of the past events.

Attaching more importance to early object relationships and the role of unconscious phantasy, Klein understands transference as rooted in primitive phantasy object relationships. Freud saw that the adult transferred his buried childish feelings on to the analyst. Klein saw the underlying baby feelings, phantasies and mechanisms. In her view, transference is based on projection and introjection. James Strachey, in "The Nature of Therapeutic

[2] Breuer and Freud, "On the Psychical Mechanism of Hysterical Phenomena: A Preliminary Communication" (1893), *SE* II, p. 7.

Action in Psychoanalysis"[3] gives the following model: the patient projects on to the analyst his superego; the analyst does not identify with it and does not act it out; his understanding modifies the superego, which can then be reintrojected in its modified form; an interpretation which achieves that is a mutative interpretation. Written in 1934, Strachey's paper takes into account Klein's work on projection and introjection. The discovery of paranoid-schizoid mechanisms and the interplay between the two positions amplified this model. The paranoid-schizoid mechanisms and manic defenses are operative in varying degrees in every analysand and manifest themselves in the transference.

The understanding of projective identification led to a greater attention to the interaction between analyst and analysand. It made the analyst more aware of what the patient projects into him, how it alters his perception of the analyst and how it influences the way he experiences the analyst's intervention. For example: if the patient is silent, he may be projecting into the analyst his experience of being a rejected and ignored child and if so, he may experience the analyst's silence as a retaliation, or the analyst's interpretation as an angry attack by a rejected child, or else as a forcible reprojection back into himself of unwanted feelings. Again, through his silence the analysand may be projecting his depression. The analyst has an apparently lifeless object on the couch and is supposed to experience the depression which, otherwise, the patient himself would have experienced, in the form of having a dead internal object. The step-by-step analysis of paranoid-schizoid and manic defenses brings the patient nearer to experiencing his own feelings and conflicts.

The analysis of the Oedipus complex, which remains

[3] *Int. J. Psycho-Anal.* 15 (1934), pp. 127–86.

central, is carried out in the same terms, taking up with great care projections and distortions, and manic and schizoid defenses against the full experience of the Oedipus complex. In certain ways the technique developed by Melanie Klein is very classical. Not only does she maintain the psychoanalytical setting as devised by Freud but she does so with particular rigor. Her technique makes this necessary because the deeper the analysis, the more important is the stability of the setting and the psychoanalytical stance of the analyst. But the content and the style of the interpretation underwent an evolution. Her views on the role played by unconscious phantasy influenced the style of interpretation. They demanded, for example, a different appraisal of reality. In classical technique there was a tendency to treat the communications of the patient about real external events as not being part of the psychoanalytical process. They refer to reality and therefore are not interpreted. Klein sees reality and phantasy as intimately interwoven. However "real" the event reported, it must be considered in its interaction with the patient's phantasy life, in order to show how unconscious phantasy influences and colors his experience of reality and how reality, in turn, may alter the phantasy. This makes the interpretation of transference more continuous and more central. In Klein's view, the relationships with internal objects are reflected in and influence all activities. Therefore, the relation to the analyst, as the representative of these objects, crucially affects all the patient's relations to reality, and so the element of the transference is important in every communication.

Kleinian technique also adopts a different approach to defenses. In classical analysis it was considered best to analyze the defenses first and to treat with great caution the conflicts and anxieties which are defended against. This, quite correctly, led to the view that it is dangerous to analyze pre-psychotics, because, once the defenses were analyzed, the patients would be flooded with primitive impulses and phantasies and would break down into a psychosis. Analyzing as Mrs. Klein did, in terms of unconscious phantasy rather than of impulse versus defense, the analyst interprets the dynamic phantasy, including the defenses and the underlying anxieties (e.g., manic phantasies and their connection with the depressive phantasies and anxieties).

The analyst's aim is to reduce the anxiety by interpreting it simultaneously with the defense. Analyzing consistently in the transference, that is, in an object relationship, makes such an approach natural. One can show the patient how he experiences a relationship which gives rise to anxiety or guilt, and how he alters it in phantasy, to avoid pain.

This approach leads also to a difference in the timing and the level of interpretation. The recommended classical approach was to proceed from the surface to the depth and from the genital to the pre-genital—pre-genital interpretations, particularly those referring to the oral phase, being considered dangerous. Klein, from the beginning of her work, aimed at interpreting at the level at which she thought anxiety was active and at which the patient operated. If a patient starts his analysis by expressing, say, fears of being sucked dry, an interpretation at the oral level seems more to the point than a more "superficial" one. If he starts by expressing fears of being invaded or unduly influenced, an interpretation at a more superficial level not only fails to relieve his anxiety but also is not, in any sense, safer. For example, if a patient is in a state of projective identification, having in phantasy projected his sexual feelings into the analyst, an Oedipal genital interpretation could well be experienced as a sexual assault. A much more primitive level of projective identification has to be interpreted before the Oedipal material can be safely approached.

The patient projects into the analyst objects which may be split or fragmented, idealized, destructive or destroyed. He also projects split-off parts of his own self. The analyst's ability to contain these projected parts, and the interpretations which connect the various elements, help the patient to bring together what has been fragmented, to reintegrate the splits, and to take back into himself parts of his own self which had been attributed to objects. All those steps bring him gradually nearer to the depressive position: that is, to the state of being an integrated self in relation to an integrated object.

This is not to say that Melanie Klein favored "here and now" interpretations (that is, interpretations of the patient's relation to the analyst only without a reference to the past—a technique used by some analysts). She always recognized that in the transference the patient projects into the analyst an internal world determined by past experiences, and past experiences revived in the transference have to be recognized in their relation to the real historical past. The past object relationships which have become the structure of the internal world are relived in the transference, and in this reliving they evolve. It is this evolution in the transference which constitutes the dynamic part of the therapeutic relationship.

The discovery of envy as an important disturbing factor in the therapeutic evolution has given psychoanalytic technique greater refinement in dealing with negative therapeutic reactions and other forms of resistance to progress. Klein's contribution has made it possible to extend the range of patients considered suitable for psychoanalysis, so that it now includes patients suffering from such conditions as borderline states between neurosis and psychosis, delinquency, psychosomatic illness, character

disorders, and so on—conditions which cannot be analyzed without an understanding of the paranoid-schizoid
mechanisms and of the role of envy. The technique for
the analysis of psychotics is still in an early phase of
development, but Klein's ideas have provided a theoretical
framework and a technical approach which makes further exploration possible.

It used to be thought that narcissistic and schizoid patients, as well as psychotics, developed no transference.
The identification of psychotic and narcissistic types of
transference, and the ability to make use of them in the
analytic setting, became possible with the understanding
of the internal object relationships, and the functioning
of projective identification underlying pathological states
of this kind.

Melanie Klein's technique is used and developed further by her immediate pupils and followers, but the
influence both of her theories and her technique has
spread well beyond those known as "Kleinians." Numer-
ous analysts now work with ideas and methods deriving
from her thought, often without being aware of the source
of these ideas.

Her influence extends also beyond the field of clinical
psychoanalysis. The concept of the two positions throws
new light on the functioning of the mind in health as well
as in pathology, and it has been usefully applied in many
fields. In the philosophy of mind it has been used to illuminate such problems as the psychological basis of ethics.
Her ideas about the growth of the mental apparatus in
terms of projection and introjection have made an impact on theories of thinking, and her work on the roots
of sublimation and creativity has given impetus to work
in the fields of art criticism and aesthetics. Her ideas
have also been applied in the fields of group relations
and sociology. Indeed, her theory, being concerned with

object relations, lends itself particularly well to the study of group phenomena. Psychoanalysts using her concepts describe groups and social institutions as organizations evolved partly to deal with individual psychotic anxieties by using common group defenses. It is possible to observe in groups the functioning of the defenses, for example to identify the working of projection in groups that idealize themselves and see all badness outside, of splitting in intragroup conflicts, of manic defenses in megalomanic groups, et cetera. Both small and large groups have been studied in this way and conclusions drawn from such work have been cautiously applied to the understanding of broader social structures.

Melanie Klein's work, from the beginning, has stimulated controversy, and criticisms have varied through the course of years. Most consistently she has been charged with attributing far too much complexity and activity to the mental life of the infant in his first two years. It was averred that this was out of keeping with the findings of neurophysiology and with such academic psychological work as that of Piaget. This criticism seems to be less well founded today when new research[4] suggests that the infant's perception and object relatedness is far greater than had been suspected.

It has also been said that her theories are not proven. Whether or not this is so depends on how one evaluates psychoanalytic evidence. Klein's work must be thought of as still in progress; and psychoanalysis as a whole is not a field in which one expects the kind of proof demanded

[4] E.g., H. R. Schaffer, *The Growth of Sociability* (Baltimore: Penguin, 1972); T. B. Brazelton, E. Tronick, L. Adamson, H. Als, and S. Weise, "Early Mother-Infant Reciprocity," *Parent-Infant Interaction*, Ciba Foundation Symposium 33 (Holland, 1975); M. R. Moore and A. N. Meltzoff, "Neonate Imitation: A Test of Existence and Mechanism," paper presented to the Society for Research in Child Development (Denver, Colorado, 1975).

in the physical sciences. Klein opened up areas of investigation into what Freud called "the dim and shadowy era" of early childhood, which is also the dim and shadowy area of the more primitive layers of the unconscious, and she has provided both a conceptual framework for understanding them and a technical tool for their investigation.

Mrs. Klein as a person is not easy to describe. Like most very creative people she was many-faceted, and accounts of her differ. She has been described by some as warm-hearted, tolerant, and good-tempered; by others as intolerant, aggressive, and demanding. She once described herself as primarily a very passionate person. She spoke of her early marriage, which put a stop to her other plans, as being due to her passionate temperament. Following the breakup of her marriage she had one long-lasting relationship, which she described as the great love of her life, but of which little is known. When she discovered psychoanalysis she became wholly committed to it, and this passion for and devotion to her work was certainly her leading characteristic. As a child and as a young woman she had been very ambitious. She thought that this was partly due to her having to fulfill Sidonie's and Emmanuel's hopes for her. But as her interest in and love for psychoanalysis grew, the wish to contribute to it and to develop it further took the place of personal ambition. It was the future of psychoanalysis, not her own ambition, that preoccupied her. She considered herself always a disciple of Freud and Abraham, and as she became more convinced of the importance and value of her work, she saw herself as their principal successor.

Melanie Klein's intense involvement in her work explains much of her character. Although she was tolerant, and could accept with an open mind the criticisms of her friends and ex-pupils, whom she often consulted, this was so only so long as one accepted the fundamental tenets of her work. If she felt this to be under attack, she could become very fierce in its defense. And if she did not get sufficient support from those she considered her friends, she could grow very bitter, sometimes in an unjust way. For instance, she received enormous support from Ernest Jones, but when the Freuds arrived in London and the Controversial Discussions took place, although intellectually she could understand Jones's difficult position, emotionally she found it hard to forgive him that he did not support her entirely. The details of her relationship with her daughter and later with Paula Heimann are not known, but her single-mindedness about her work may have contributed to the bitterness which developed between her and her daughter and to the disagreements with Paula Heimann.

Though easy to get on with in her private life, she brooked no compromise about her work. She was very clear in her mind about it. She said once that compromise was necessary and useful in political matters within a psychoanalytical society as well as in the world; but there could be no compromise in scientific matters. The best one can do is to keep an open mind and admit the possibility of being wrong, but one cannot pretend that things can be "a bit like this and a bit like that" in order to appease or placate an opponent. But although she valued open-mindedness, she was thoroughly convinced of the rightness of her approach and found it disappointing when others did not agree with her. To the end of her life she felt a little bewildered and deeply hurt by Freud's coolness toward her and her work, which she saw as being close to his. Believing that she had developed it in the same ethos and further than any other living analyst, she found it very difficult to bear that he did not see it that way. She understood it intellectually, but she found it hard to accept that Freud would naturally be more disposed to support his own daughter.

Klein expected a very high standard of work from herself and from others, and was most impatient of sloppiness and excuses for bad work. She could become quite scathing. At an international congress a psychoanalyst spoke at great length about the dangers of the analyst falling in with the patient's idealization of her. Mrs. Klein replied saying that if Dr. X took a bit more trouble in understanding the paranoid anxieties and the negative transference underlying such an idealization of herself, she would not feel so much at risk of self-idealization. On another occasion in the British Society, there was a discussion in which it was argued that the analyst must not aim at being perfect—that it was good for the patient to discover the failings of the analyst, and that the mistakes of the analyst promoted the development of the patient. Mrs. Klein said that her colleagues must feel very near perfection if they thought their failings and mistakes were such a matter for self-congratulation. As for herself, she found that even if she tried her best, she made quite enough mistakes as it was; and when accuesd of perfectionism, she said it was not a matter of not making mistakes—everybody makes mistakes—but of recognizing mistakes for what they were and trying to correct them, the important thing being not to elevate mistakes into theories. She was generally very outspoken in her criticisms, and this did not always make her popular.

What struck one most in her as a private person was her warmth and her quite extraordinary vitality, which remained with her to the end of her life. During her last summer she told only very few friends about her state of fatigue and the doctor's diagnosis of overwork. They were very worried and wanted to have a second opinion, because, despite her age, they knew that this was out of character. In the event they were right.

As a young woman she must have suffered from depression, but she seldom spoke of it. What first brought her to analysis was both the enormous interest aroused in her by reading Freud, and, from the therapeutic point of view, an awareness of her depression. But from the time she came to London it would have been difficult to guess that. She was full of vigor and interests. Though working very hard both with her patients and with her writing, she maintained her involvement in reading, in music, and in travel. She was full of surprises, and could give her attention to most unexpected matters. One day a colleague was asked by a French winegrower if he knew a psychoanalyst in London called Melanie Klein. Startled by this inquiry, he asked how the man came to know about her, and found out that Mrs. Klein was remembered in that region of France as the only woman ever to have won a wine-tasting competition. When Mrs. Klein was told about it, she said that her father had had an interest in wine and that she had kept it up.

But her main interest was always in people. With her friends she was warm and affectionate and full of *joie de vivre*. Even in her old age she was always ready to respond to an invitation to a party, a movie, or a theater. She enjoyed company and shared intellectual and artistic interests. She was also very feminine and could be quite coquettish, even in her old age. As a young woman she was described by those who knew her as very beautiful. Michael Balint said that she was known in the Berlin psychoanalytical circle as "the black beauty." As an old woman, she retained her beauty and a trace of feminine vanity. She took great trouble with her clothes, and it was a joke among her friends that the moment her Congress paper was ready, she would turn all her attention to choosing her Congress hat, and wanted her friends to take nearly as much notice of the hat as of the paper. But she was not egocentric. Her interest in people made her into a very good listener, and she always found time to be available to her friends when they needed help. She enjoyed particularly good contact with children and with babies. She loved visiting people who had babies, and could spend a long time with a baby "listening" to it.

She was a person who aroused strong emotions. She received a great deal of love and affection from her friends and close colleagues, and often inspired passionate devotion. Her uncompromising attitude about her work made her many enemies, but she was a powerful personality and commanded almost universal respect.

SHORT BIBLIOGRAPHY

WORKS BY MELANIE KLEIN

The works are ordered by date of first publication, and the number of the volume in which they appear in *The Writings of Melanie Klein* (London: Hogarth Press, 1975) is given in square brackets.

1921 "The Development of a Child." *Imago* 7 [I]
1922 "Inhibitions and Difficulties in Puberty." *Die neue Erziehung 4.* [I]
1923 "The Role of the School in the Libidinal Development of the Child." *Int. Z. f. Psychoanal. 9.* [I]
"Early Analysis." *Imago 9.* [I]
1925 "A Contribution to the Psychogenesis of Tics." *Int. Z. f. Psychoanal. 11.* [I]
1926 "The Psychological Principles of Early Analysis." *Int. J. Psycho-Anal. 7.* [I]
1927 "Symposium on Child Analysis." *Int. J. Psycho-Anal. 8.* [I]
"Criminal Tendencies in Normal Children." *Brit J. Med. Psychol. 7.* [I]
1928 "Early Stages of the Oedipus Conflict." *Int. J. Psycho-Anal. 9.* [I]

1929 "Personification in the Play of Children." *Int. J. Psycho-Anal. 10.* [I]
"Infantile Anxiety Situations Reflected in a Work of Art and in the Creative Impulse." *Int. J. Psycho-Anal. 10.* [I]

1930 "The Importance of Symbol-Formation in the Development of the Ego." *Int. J. Psycho-Anal. 11.* [I]
The Psychotherapy of the Psychoses." *Brit. J. Med. Psychol. 10.* [I]

1931 "A Contribution to the Theory of Intellectual Inhibition." *Int. J. Psycho-Anal. 12.* [I]

1932 *The Psycho-Analysis of Children.* London: Hogarth Press [II]; New York: Delacorte, 1975.

1933 "The Early Development of Conscience in the Child." *Psychoanalysis Today,* New York: Covici-Friede [I]

1934 "On Criminality." *Brit. J. Med. Psychol. 14.* [I]

1935 "A Contribution to the Psychogenesis of Manic-Depressive States." *Int. J. Psycho-Anal. 16.* [I]

1936 "Weaning." *On the Bringing Up of Children,* ed. Rickman. London: Kegan Paul. [I]

1937 "Love, Guilt and Reparation." *Love, Hate and Reparation,* with Riviere, London: Hogarth Press [I]; New York: Norton, 1964.

1940 "Mourning and Its Relation to Manic-Depressive States." *Int. J. Psycho-Anal. 21.* [I]

1945 "The Oedipus Complex in the Light of Early Anxieties." *Int. J. Psycho-Anal. 26.* [I]

1946 "Notes on Some Schizoid Mechanisms." *Int. J. Psycho-Anal. 27.* [III]

1948 *Contributions to Psycho-Analysis 1921–1945.* London: Hogarth Press. [I]
"On the Theory of Anxiety and Guilt." *Int. J. Psycho-Anal. 29.* [III]

1950 "On the Criteria for the Termination of a Psycho-Analysis." *Int. J. Psycho-Anal. 31.* [III]

1952 "The Origins of Transference." *Int. J. Psycho-Anal. 33.* [III]
"The Mutual Influences in the Development of Ego and Id." *Psychoanal. Study Child 7.* [III]
"Some Theoretical Conclusions Regarding the Emotional Life of the Infant." *Development in Psycho-Analysis,* with Heimann, Isaacs, and Riviere. London: Hogarth Press. [III]
"On Observing the Behaviour of Young Infants." Ibid. [III]

1955 "The Psycho-Analytic Play Technique: Its History and Significance." *New Directions in Psycho-Analysis.* London: Tavistock. [III]
"On Identification." Ibid. [III]

1957 *Envy and Gratitude.* London: Tavistock [III]; New York: Delacorte, 1975.

1958 "On the Development of Mental Functioning." *Int. J. Psycho-Anal. 29. [III]*

1959 "Our Adult World and Its Roots in Infancy." *Hum. Relations 12.* [III]

1960 "A Note on Depression in the Schizophrenic." *Int. J. Psycho-Anal. 41.* [III]
"On Mental Health." *Brit. J. Med. Psychol. 33.* [III]

1961 *Narrative of a Child Psycho-Analysis.* London: Hogarth Press [IV]; New York: Delacorte, 1975.

1963 "Some Reflections on *The Oresteia." Our Adult World and Other Essays.* London: Heinemann Medical. [III]
"On the Sense of Loneliness." Ibid. [III]

WORKS BY OTHERS

Abraham, Karl. "A Short Study of the Development of the Libido, Viewed in the Light of Mental Disorders" (1924), in *The Selected Papers of Karl Abraham.* London: Hogarth Press, 1927.

Freud, Sigmund. *The Standard Edition of the Complete Psychological Works of Sigmund Freud.* James Strachey, general editor, in collaboration with Anna Freud, assisted by Alix Strachey and Alan Tyson. London: Hogarth Press, 1963–74; New York: Macmillan, 1974. The following works are referred to in this book (*Standard Edition* volume numbers in brackets):
"On the Psychical Mechanism of Hysterical Phenomena: A Preliminary Communication" (1893). With Joseph Breuer. [II]
On Dreams (1901). [V]; New York: Norton, 1963.
The Psychopathology of Everyday Life (1901). [VI]; New York: Norton, 1971.
"Fragment of an Analysis of a Case of Hysteria" (1905). [VII]
"Analysis of a Phobia in a Five-Year-Old Boy" (1909). [X]
"Psycho-Analytic Notes upon an Autobiographical Account of a Case of Paranoia (Dementia Paranoides)" (1911). [XII]; New York: Basic Books, 1959.

"Formulations Regarding the Two Principles of Mental Functioning" (1911). [XII]

"On Narcissism: An Introduction" (1914). [XIV]

"Instincts and Their Vicissitudes" (1915). [XIV]

"Mourning and Melancholia" (1917). [XIV]

"Introductory Lectures on Psycho-Analysis" (1916–17). [XV, XVI]; New York: Liveright, 1977.

"From the History of an Infantile Neurosis" (1918). [XVII]

"Beyond the Pleasure Principle" (1920). [XVIII]; New York: Norton, 1963.

"The Ego and the Id" (1923). [XIX]; New York: Norton, 1962.

"The Economic Problem of Masochism" (1924). [XIX]

"Negation" (1925). [XIX]

"Some Psychical Consequences of the Anatomical Distinction between the Sexes" (1925). [XIX]

"Inhibitions, Symptoms and Anxiety" (1926). [XX]

"Civilization and Its Discontents" (1930). [XXI]

"Female Sexuality" (1931). [XXI]

"New Introductory Lectures on Psycho-Analysis" (1933). [XXII]

"An Outline of Psycho-Analysis" (1940). [XXIII]

"Splitting of the Ego in the Process of Defense" (1940). [XXIII]

A *Psycho-Analytic Dialogue: The Letters of Sigmund Freud and Karl Abraham.* Hilda C. Abraham and Ernst L. Freud, eds. London: Hogarth Press, 1965.

Freud, Anna. *The Psycho-Analytical Treatment of Children.* London: Imago, 1946–56.

Jones, Ernest. "The Theory of Symbolism"; "Early Female Sexuality"; and "Female Sexuality," in *Papers on Psycho-Analysis* (fifth ed.). London: Ballière, Tindall, and Cox, 1948.

Wollheim, Richard. *Sigmund Freud* (Modern Masters series). New York: The Viking Press, 1971.

INDEX

I.th. an elementary, unnecessary summary
of Freud's translation develop[ment]

II   The Safe or M. W.
            Death of Falle, Safe, Frocke, Analyst

         Budapest, Berlin, London
                                    1927
III Fritz u. Rita: Play, analysis.

    How can they — Kl. K + Anna F. -
make over the others' softly responsible
Perth necessary?

Melanie Klein

Hanna Segal

Melanie Klein's pioneering work in the psychoanalysis of the child, made possible by the "play technique" she developed for working with very young children, has yielded insights into the earliest and most basic psychic states. Her writings on topics such as mourning, guilt, anxiety, paranoia, and schizophrenia have been influential in theoretical and practical psychology. In this book, the first short introduction to a very important body of work, Hanna Segal—herself an eminent psychoanalyst and a former colleague of Klein's—traces the development of Klein's ideas within the historical context of the early years of psychoanalysis, showing where she followed and where she departed from Freud, and portrays her as a woman of great insight and originality. Dr. Segal also discusses Kleinian psychology today and its application to such areas as ethics, aesthetics, and group theory.